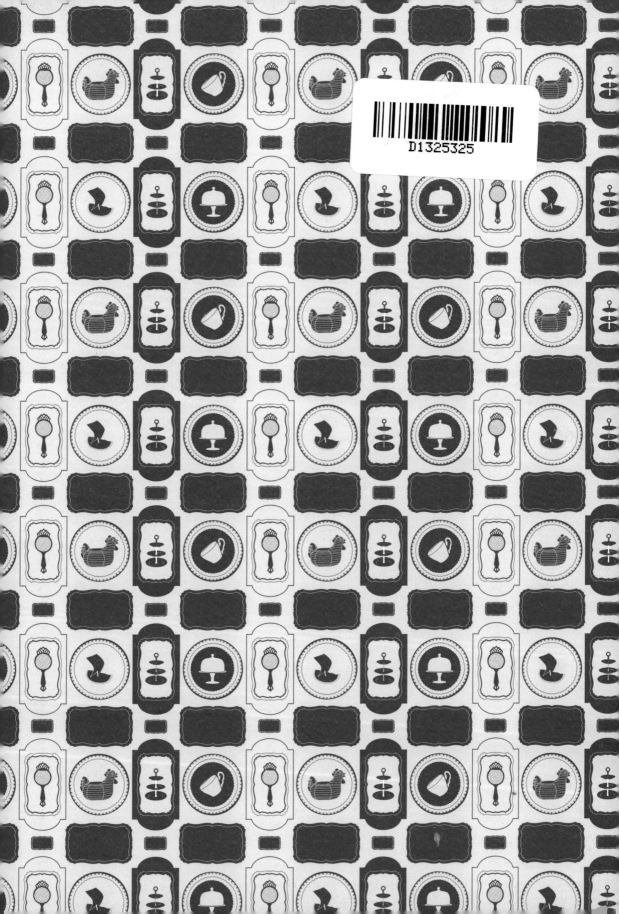

Apron Strings

—RECIPES—

from a

FAMILY KITCHEN

APRON STRINGS
First published 2013
by New Island
2 Brookside
Dundrum Road
Dublin 14

www.newisland.ie

PRINT ISBN: 978-1-84840-241-6
EPUB ISBN: 978-1-84840-242-3
MOBI ISBN: 978-1-84840243-0

Typeset by Nina Lyons
Cover design by Nina Lyons
Photography © Nessa Robins, except p 17, 236,
243, 248/249 & 256 © Diarmuid O'Donovan
Front cover Photo © Diarmuid O'Donovan
Food Stylist, Nessa Robins
Printed by Bell & Bain ltd. Scotland

10 9 8 7 6 5 4 3 2 1

NEW ISLAND

*This book is
dedicated
with love to the
memory of my
parents,*
Dermot & Bernadette
—— ROBINS ——

ACKNOWLEDGEMENTS

I would like to thank the team at New Island but especially Eoin Purcell. It is by far one of the greatest compliments for any blogger to receive an email from a publisher wondering if they'd consider writing a book based on their blog. Thank you, Eoin, for your valued support and for encouraging me to write a cookbook which is so close to my heart. I'm truly honoured to work with you.

It was my eldest boy, Jack, who set up my blog at age seven. In the early days he was most certainly my biggest encouragement. He's the best in-house tech-support that anyone could ask for. Without your involvement, Jack, the blog may never have developed as well as it did. Thank you for always finding a solution to my technical problems.

There is a wonderful community of food lovers and food bloggers online. Little did I know when I hit publish on my first blog post, back in January 2010, that I would be embarking on such an exciting foodie adventure. I have made many good friends and I'm ever grateful for the continued support of my fellow bloggers.

I'd like to give a heartfelt thank you to all my blog readers. I truly appreciate that you read the blog and thank you for your feedback and kind comments.

A big thank you to Nina Lyons, who is responsible for the wonderfully creative design of the book. I absolutely love how you have brought my photos and text together.

To my family, friends and sisters for their fantastic support, but especially Fiona and Dervilla, who were always there to give a helping hand when I was balancing book writing with family life.

To my beautiful children Jack, Tiarnán, Fionn and Millie. You are such a valued part of this book. For being almost always willing to stand and wait while Mammy caught the perfect shot for each photo, before dinners were plated up. Thank you for your help and patience. I love you dearly.

Even though my Dad passed away last December, five weeks after I handed in the text for this book, I can't do my acknowledgements without including him. He sat through endless auctions to bid for that perfect plate or bowl, which he considered would be placed well in one of my photos. Even when his mobility was poor he made his way to his tunnels to plant numerous pots of herbs for me to photograph and use in my recipes. I loved that he had such a keen interest in my life and in this book. Dad, I pray that you are at rest and know how truly grateful I am for all you did for me. Rest in peace.

Finally to my fantastic husband Diarmuid, for being my kitchen helper, my assistant food-stylist and photographer but mostly for always making me believe that I can do whatever I put my mind to. Without your constant love and endless support this book would never have been possible.

CONTENTS

Housekeeper's
~ CUT ~
20

BAKED WITH
LOVE
49

In the Family Way

88

HOST
with the
Most
110

CHILDREN'S
BIRTHDAY
Party
142

Home
NURSE
170

FOOD
for the
GREAT
OUTDOORS
192

LIFE BEYOND THE
KITCHEN
WINDOW
214

INTRODUCTION

It's Sunday morning, 8 a.m., and I have just popped a loaf of white soda into the oven, coffee is brewing and I'm looking forward to pouring myself a cup. There is something so perfect about that first cup of coffee. Somehow, once sipped, many tasks can be completed. I particularly need its encouragement this morning because, today, I am attempting to start this book.

I'm going to begin by letting you in on what has shaped me into the person who's writing this book. Primarily it will be a collection of my family favourite recipes, but also I want to include little tips and advice on how to run a home efficiently, and more important, happily. I spend most of my days at home, with the children, baking, cooking, collecting eggs and rummaging through the garden to see what I'll make for dinner. This lifestyle, that I wholeheartedly embrace, wasn't planned, it just simply evolved. It grew through my love of food and the desire to feed my family well. When I was given the opportunity to spend more time in my kitchen I loved it, and food started to play a much greater role in our lives. I certainly don't want to convey that I have the picture-perfect family; believe me there are often days that we are at loggerheads, and the worry of a sick family member can often shadow out happiness, but normally life is good and overall we feel content and happy in our days together. I'm a true believer that facing each day with positivity can change your world. Even if there is sadness in your heart, over time positivity can come from a negative experience. For me, it came from the untimely death of my mother. It took time, but eventually I knew that I didn't want to waste a moment with any unnecessary worries, but to focus more on what I really wanted from life, and top of this list was to raise happy children in an encouraging and contented home environment.

Each and every day I love to be kept busy. I expect, in some ways, this may come from my mother. She was always busy and forever cooking. She would be ever vigilant to everyone who stepped inside her kitchen. It's often said that as we get older the similarities between us and our parents become more evident. So if this is where my busy ways come from, I'm glad that I'm nurturing them. A few years ago we built our new home and I took on the role of the project manager. It was a job that fitted me like a glove, I needed many lists, numerous phone numbers and I had plenty of figures to play around with. What may have seemed like a tremendous task to undertake wasn't and I thoroughly enjoyed it. I was in control and this suited me, to be in control was good. While the build was in progress, I was pregnant with my third child, Fionn, and working part-time as a practice nurse, but everything seemed truly manageable because I was completely in charge. I knew my schedule and what needed to be done, and was grateful that I was feeling fairly healthy. I could easily manage all. Maybe if I were given these roles to play a few years previous I would have found the stress immense and the tasks impossible. At this time, however, everything seemed doable, as there was something much graver happening in my life, which I couldn't take charge over, and this was my mother's sickness. The day Tiarnán, my second child, was born, she was diagnosed with Multiple Myeloma, a form of cancer that affects the bone marrow. Being by my mother's side throughout her illness, seeing her pain and the feeling of helplessness, made me realise what real stress was. Prior to this I wasn't a terribly stressed person anyway, yet different things would irritate me and some things could get me down. Not any more, nothing seemed important. One of the most valuable people in my life was desperately sick and there was nothing I could do about it. I wanted to remain strong and I knew that I needed to do anything I could to make each day a little better for my mother. I was twenty-nine years of age and for the first time ever in my life our roles were reversed. My mother now needed my care and my attention. I had to be there for her, just like she was always there for me. Her boots were big to fill as she, like so many mothers, had a natural touch for making a situation seem better than it was. I wasn't sure if I could offer her the same, but I certainly wanted to try.

I wasn't an amazing cook, and actually, if the truth were told, I was barely an average cook. I always enjoyed my meals and appreciated good quality food, but life was so busy that I rarely had the opportunity to spend hours in the kitchen, and I only occasionally

baked. In my mother's final few months I was grateful to spend most of my time by her side. Whenever I could, I would cook for her. A home-cooked meal from Mam had always made me feel better in the past, and I wanted it to do the same for her. This was when I started to become comfortable in the kitchen. I felt safe in the kitchen, I was doing some good. I had a role then, and when I was busy there was little time to get upset as I needed to stay strong. In the past five years I have barely left the kitchen, and not because I'm holding back on outside experiences but more because this is where I like to be and where I feel most comfortable, with my family surrounding me. In some ways I feel closest to my mother with a mixing bowl in my hand when I can't but let the happy memories from our life together come flooding back.

The last conversation I ever had with my mother was one of thanks. She thanked me for the care I gave her, and Diarmuid for running the home while I would spend hours on end by her side. In turn I assured her there was no need for thanks as it was a privilege to take care of her after all she had given me throughout my life. That night, on the car journey home from the hospital, I cried hard thinking over our words, not knowing at that moment that these would be the last words we would ever speak to each other. We knew how much we loved each other, but I'm ever so glad that we said these words, as in my grief they have given me great comfort and have taught me to appreciate those closest to me.

My mother passed away on the 10th of February 2007 at the age of 69. After she passed, I felt as if my complete life had crashed in front of me. I remember, about three months after her death, remarking to Diarmuid that I wasn't having a passing moment without thinking of her. The pain was so great that I genuinely thought that never again could I be truly happy. I was constantly being reassured by friends or family who had been grief stricken in the past that this pain would ease and that the passing of time is a great healer, but it wasn't healing for me. I loved my mother with all my heart, we were best friends, I shared everything with her, and barely a few hours passed without us chatting. But I need to tell you, especially anyone who's in that place of immense, grief-laden pain, that the pain does begin to ease. I gained strength, and as my pain eased I began to feel very grateful for this beautiful lady who was my mother. I found happiness in my memories and I would constantly remind myself of how lucky I was to have had such an amazing relationship with my mother, whom I loved so dearly. When I'd hear of a tragedy, either locally or on the news, I would be thankful that my mother's last moments were spent with her family surrounding her. She was a religious lady and she leaned heavily on her faith, especially during her sickness. Throughout my life, whenever I was upset she would always be there to remind me that someone else had a heavier cross to bear and to be ever grateful for what I have. It was her words that would echo through my thoughts as I'd feel sorry for myself. It was her positive energy that eventually helped me through my grief. I was grateful for my healthy children, my kind husband and my Dad, whom I knew needed me now more than ever before.

It was when we moved into our new home, after the birth of Fionn, that my whole life started to change. My home workload was now much greater, we had three children aged 5 and under and I also now had my Dad to consider. Previous to this I would work the days that Diarmuid was off. Even though I thoroughly enjoyed my work as a nurse, and found the change from minding the children and taking care of the home to working in a busy surgery quite refreshing, my home circumstances had changed and for me to actually close the door behind me and head to work would be difficult. Either way, I was really enjoying being at home; I was cooking and baking more than ever before. I had a new routine, which was heavily focused on food and meal times. Each morning, after the school run, I would make home-made soda bread with Tiarnán and then we'd start to prepare the day's meals. I always seemed to be busy, the children were content and this was comforting. The running of a busy house, with many visitors in and out, really suited me. With all that in mind we decided that I would take a short break from nursing, at least until everyone was a little older and more settled.

About a year after my Mam passed away, I started to become really aware of how lucky I was. The stress of a loved one being sick, and the possibility of them dying, is so intense that, since going through this with my mother, minor incidentals in day-to-day life can rarely upset me. I made a conscious decision to try and enjoy every day to the full, to approach each day with a positive outlook and to always be grateful for my good fortune. There is a lot of joy to be gained from cooking for loved ones. Food has always played a major role in our home. My mother was a wonderful cook and the happiest of times were, and still are, spent chatting around the kitchen table while diving into something delicious. Throughout the book I would like to share some of my family's favourite recipes. Most are suited for everyday meals, some for times of celebration while others will serve well when someone in the family is under the weather. What I cook for my family is very much guided by what is in season, so many of my recipes are influenced from outside the kitchen; my hens, garden and foraging all play a great part in what I cook from day to day.

I'm privileged to have some very precious people in my life who have impacted on me so strongly and continue to nurture my positive outlook. None more important than my four beautiful children, who are a constant reminder to me that life is good and the world that we live in can be a very exciting and wonderful place. We all know of someone who has made a difference to our lives, and most times we don't need to leave our homes to find those whose influence upon us is the greatest. I'd like this book to be a celebration of family while giving a glimpse into my life as a fairly happy home-maker.

CONVERSION
CHARTS

TEMPERATURE

CENTIGRADE	FAHRENHEIT	GAS MARK	DESCRIPTION
140°C	275°F	1	Very Cool
150°C	300°F	2	Cool
160°C	325°F	3	Fairly Warm
180°C	350°F	4	Warm
190°C	375°F	5	Moderate
200°C	400°F	6	Fairly Hot
220°C	425°F	7	Hot
230°C	450°F	8	Very Hot
240°C	475°F	9	Extremely Hot

The oven settings here are only approximate, and individual cookers may vary.

Please note that all recipes in this book were tested in a fan-assisted oven. If using a conventional oven, remember to increase the temperature and cooking time accordingly.

WEIGHTS

METRIC	IMPERIAL	METRIC	IMPERIAL
10g	½oz	150g	5oz
20g	¾oz	175g	6oz
25g	1oz	200g	7oz
40g	1½oz	225g	8oz
50g	2oz	250g	9oz
60g	2½oz	275g	10oz
75g	3oz	350g	12
100g	3½oz	450g	1lb
110g	4oz	700g	1½lbs
125g	4½oz	900g	2lbs
		1.35kg	3lbs

VOLUME

METRIC	IMPERIAL
2.5ml	½ teaspoon (tsp)
5ml	1tsp
15ml	1tablespoon (tbsp)
30ml	1 fl oz
55ml	2 fl oz
75ml	3 fl oz
100ml	¼ pint
275ml	½ pint
570ml	1 pint
725ml	1¼ pints
1L	1¾ pints
1.2L	2 pints
1.5L	2½ pints
2.25L	4 pints

Housekeeper's
~ CUT ~

When money was scarce, the ability to be self-sufficient and make do with what was accessible was essential. My father's tales of his childhood are full of pride. He tells of how little everybody had, but yet despite this hardship they never went hungry.

A lot of credit has to be given to the women of that time. They may have been perceived as having the less important role in society, yet behind the scenes their role was so much greater than was ever acknowledged. We are so accustomed to reading about the subservient roles of women by comparison to their breadwinning husbands and fathers, but the fact remains that there would have been no bread made whatsoever if it weren't for these humble ladies. Naturally I jest, but at a time when survival was at the top of the agendas of most individuals, daily life was guided by the need to find food and nourishment for feeding one's family.

In rural Ireland work was scarce, but if a family didn't have access to land they would help out a neighbouring farm, and in exchange for their time they would receive essentials such as milk, butter and potatoes. Housewives had limited supplies to work with, and so naturally they needed to make the most of every piece of food available to them. The cheaper cuts of meats were valued, and slow cooking of food was favoured. Ingredients were cherished and food, no matter what, was always enjoyed.

Even though I'm not so sure if I could survive without some of my kitchen luxuries, there really is so much that we in modern society can learn from the housewives of years ago. These ladies managed their kitchens like businesses, and looking back their ways were extremely enterprising.

THRIFTY TIPS FOR RUNNING A HOUSEHOLD

Much money is needed to run a home these days, and one of the greatest expenditures is on food. In today's society it can be an awful lot easier to shop for cheap, nutrient-poor foods than for high-quality and nutrient-rich ones. As consumers we are bombarded with choice. Big companies have the money to promote their products, and often what is on special offer at our supermarket may not be the healthy option. Many of our basic foods aren't the expensive ones, and if only we had the willpower to only pick up what we truly need in a week, all sorts of savings could be made. There are a few steps that I have found to reduce our household spending, which I try to incorporate into running the family home:

- Check the store cupboard before shopping. I often have four packets of pasta in the press only to return home with two more.

- Rotate the food in the store cupboards and fridge, putting the freshest food at the back.

- A shopping list is of paramount importance for not overspending. Make this list over the week, jotting down items that are needed for your press.

- Try to buy unpackaged fruit and vegetables. You can more easily check their freshness, and also cut down on packaging waste.

- I always shop for meat and fish with my local butcher. The price is no more expensive than the supermarket equivalent, and also the quality of the meat is exceptional. These are knowledgeable men, and are always worth having a chat with. Their expertise can easily guide on the cheaper cuts of meat, that when tenderly cooked will produce an economically impressive, tasty dish. They also have lovely sharp knives that will prepare your meat ready for cooking in minutes, which will save you time when cooking the dinner.

✤ After having a roast chicken for dinner, pop the carcass into a pot of cold water along with an onion, a stick of celery, a few carrots, a couple of bay leaves and some black pepper. After bubbling away for a couple of hours this will produce a rich, flavoursome stock that can be cooled and frozen for using in a future stock-based dish.

✤ Meat will often be the most expensive component of a dish. To bulk up a meal and make it more substantially filling, pack it with extra vegetables or beans and lentils. Or dare I say {without my father listening}, have a few meat-free days each week.

✤ Buy and cook with foods that are in season. These will often be cheaper to buy and taste a lot better than the out-of-season variety that have been flown many miles to make it to our plates.

✤ I know I certainly fall into that 'buy one get one free' pit, whereby I pick up maybe discounted biscuits on the premise of having them in the press for a visitor, but simply can't resist once my night time cuppa needs some company. These special offers can sometimes seem too good to resist, but in recent times I've considered only picking up foods on offer that are normally a part of my weekly shop, though this sometimes can be rather difficult.

✤ Every supermarket will have a different cheese, bread, yogurt etc. on offer each week. If what is discounted is equivalent to your normal purchase, then cross brands depending on what is on offer.

✤ Real butter can be an expensive ingredient, so when you find it on offer buy in bulk and freeze for up to six months.

✤ Milk can also be frozen for up to six months, so having a few bottles in the freezer can save money, especially if you've to drive to the shop solely for the morning's milk.

✤ Having our own vegetable garden has certainly cut down on some cost. Not everyone has the space or time for a garden, but even a few containers on the window-sill and a packet of lettuce seeds will keep you in lettuce for many weeks.

✤ I bake quite a bit, and also cook many dishes containing eggs. Having my own hens has saved me some money over the years.

✤ Often the leftovers from a meal can taste better the next day. Reheat if necessary, or try to incorporate them into another dish.

❀ I had difficulty getting one of my boys to eat the crusts from their bread. What an awful waste to throw these out, so while I went through a phase of cutting off the perimeter of each sandwich, I would make them into breadcrumbs by whizzing them up in the food processor, and then popping them into the freezer.

❀ Using fresh, nutritious ingredients is what will save us the most in the long term, as there is a definite link between the foods we eat and the health of our bodies.

Cooking can sometimes truly fascinate me, as it never fails to amaze me how a few simple ingredients can so easily be transformed into a taste sensation. This soup, based on the simplest of ingredients: potatoes and onions, is a good example of this. A little butter is enough to give a buttery sheen to the vegetables before cooking them in a simmering stock. A really good soup greatly benefits from a well-flavoured stock. Home-made is generally best, but there are also many good-quality stocks available to buy.

With many soups the option to purée or leave some chunks floating is normally a personal choice, but I would certainly urge you to go with the puréed option for this soup. When blended the high quantity of potatoes lends to a silky smooth sheen, resulting in a velvety rich soup. I quite like the addition of something crunchy to contrast with the smoothness of the soup, so topping with a little fried chorizo, with its smoky tones, complements this soup beautifully. Alternatively, the soup could be garnished with some finely chopped chives and crunchy croutons for that added bite.

WHITE ONION, POTATO & CHORIZO SOUP

INGREDIENTS

50g butter

250g white onions, roughly chopped

450g potatoes, peeled and diced

Salt and freshly ground pepper

5 sprigs of thyme, leaves only

1lt chicken stock

75ml milk

75ml cream

To Serve:

100g chorizo, cut into thin slices, then quartered

2tbsp cream

METHOD

Melt the butter in a large saucepan. When it begins to foam, add the onions and potatoes, and stir to combine with the butter.

Sprinkle with a little salt, a few grinds of pepper and the thyme leaves. Place a butter wrapper or a piece of greaseproof paper over the vegetables to help them sweat. Cover with the lid of the saucepan. Sweat over a low heat for about 10 minutes, making sure the vegetables don't stick to the bottom of the saucepan.

When the vegetables are soft but not coloured, add the stock and continue to cook for another 15 mins until the vegetables are soft.

Using a hand blender or a food processor, purée the soup until it is smooth. Taste, and season if necessary. Pour in the milk and cream and stir well to combine.

Heat a frying pan and fry the chorizo slices for 2 minutes on each side.

Pour the soup into serving bowls and garnish each with a few slices of cooked chorizo and a little drizzle of cream.

Serves 6

As I'm lucky enough to have access to a local butcher who sells Irish-reared free-range chicken at an affordable price, we have many mid-week dinners that are chicken based. Everyone has a couple of dishes that are regularly on their weekly menu, and this happens to be one of mine. As with most dishes, I don't stick stringently to the ingredients list; if I'm short on spinach I may add some mange-tout, and if I don't have crème fraiche I may substitute it with something like mascarpone, sour cream or a little fresh cream. The pine nuts add a satisfying crunch but can be omitted, especially if serving to children. I often have picky eaters at my table, and even though I wouldn't necessarily place my father in this category he certainly wouldn't consider that he'd had his dinner unless there were potatoes somewhere in the mix. Boiling up a few spuds can be a lot easier than making a whole separate meal, so the fantastic thing about this dish is that it not only works well served with rice or pasta but is also well paired with a few auld reliable potatoes. The sauce is mouth-wateringly creamy, which makes for a very luxurious but quick to make mid-week meal.

CHICKEN IN A HERBY WHITE WINE SAUCE

INGREDIENTS

Knob of butter

1 tbsp olive oil

4 chicken fillets, diced

Salt and freshly
  ground pepper

1 onion, finely diced

3 cloves of garlic,
  crushed

300ml stock

200ml white wine

125g crème fraiche

50g pine nuts

100g spinach leaves

1 tbsp chopped parsley

Handful of basil leaves,
  torn into pieces

To Serve:

Boiled Rice /
  Steamed Potatoes
  / Cooked Pasta

METHOD

Heat a large frying pan and add a drizzle
of olive oil and the knob of butter.

Add the diced chicken, season with a little sea
salt and freshly ground pepper. Cook for about
5 minutes until it is sealed and browned.

Add the onion and cook until they are soft but not coloured.
Stir in the garlic and continue to cook for a minute.

Pour in the stock, white wine and crème fraiche.
Leave to simmer, on a low heat, for 20 minutes.

In a frying pan, lightly toast the pine nuts for
a minute and then leave to one side.

Just before serving, but still on the heat, stir in the spinach,
parsley and basil, then sprinkle over the pine nuts.

Serve immediately with rice, pasta or potatoes.

Serves 4

While tucking into this dish, even on a cold winter's day, it will always remind me of holidaying in Spain. The flavours are so distinctively Mediterranean, and even though it is characteristically a stew, I would still wholeheartedly enjoy this dish in the summer months. It's a wonderfully comforting dish that gives a mighty burst of internal heat thanks to the chorizo and chilli. It's also a real favourite of mine because it can be made solely from store cupboard ingredients. Chorizo is a fabulous ingredient to have on standby, as it has a good shelf life and is just so versatile. It works as a wonderful base for many pasta sauces, and is especially good in this soup, as the other ingredients get the benefit of being seared in its robust, smoky flavoured oil.

CHORIZO, BEAN & PASTA SOUP

INGREDIENTS

200g chorizo, cut into chunks

2 onions, finely chopped

1 carrot, diced

1 small red chilli, finely chopped

3 cloves of garlic, crushed

½tsp cumin

1tsp smoked paprika

Black pepper

1 yellow pepper, finely sliced

1 tin tomatoes

1tsp tomato purée

500ml vegetable stock

1 tin of mixed beans, rinsed & drained

400g cooked pasta

METHOD

To a large saucepan add the chorizo and fry for a couple of minutes, just until some of the oil has begun to come from the chorizo.

Scoop out the chorizo and leave on a plate. Then add the onions and carrot to this flavoursome oil. On a medium heat, fry gently for a couple of minutes.

Add to this the chilli, garlic, cumin, smoked paprika and a twist of black pepper. Stir together for 1 minute allowing the spices to toast a little.

Add the pepper, tomatoes, tomato purée, vegetable stock and mixed beans.

Simmer for 25–30 minutes. Add the cooked pasta for the final 2 minutes. Check the seasoning then serve with some crusty fresh bread.

Serves 4–6

We all know that children can slightly exaggerate their feelings of hunger when waiting for their next meal to be served, yet we have all been in that situation ourselves where we are sitting in a restaurant and minutes feel like hours because our hungry tummies are so eagerly awaiting some food. When preparing the family dinner, to counteract the stomping of feet, I sometimes try to distract my hungry little monsters by delegating a few jobs. I must warn you that this may not always work, but if it is something fun, like rolling meatballs as in this recipe, well… it can prove quite successful. I wouldn't, however, allocate two hungry helpers to this task, as the likelihood of sausage meat being flung at the wall would be a real possibility.

I tend to keep the meatballs relatively small, about a teaspoon full of meat is sufficient, and then simply roll into a ball. A bowl of water comes in very handy for dipping hands into between the making of each meatball. All the ingredients, apart from the sausages, can be in the store cupboard, so this is a wonderfully convenient recipe to have at hand. As an alternative, you could make beef meatballs using my beefburger recipe, and just shape accordingly. These, too, are delicious with the thick and rich tomato sauce.

SAUSAGE MEATBALLS WITH A TOMATO & RED WINE SAUCE

INGREDIENTS

10 good quality sausages

1 tbsp olive oil

500g spaghetti

1 onion, finely chopped

2 cloves of garlic, crushed

2 tins of cherry tomatoes

100ml red wine

1 tsp dried herbs

2 tbsp sugar

Sea salt & freshly ground pepper

To Serve:

Parmesan cheese

Crusty bread

METHOD

Snip the sausages apart and squeeze out the meat into a large bowl. Using wet hands roll the mixture into about 20 meatballs.

Heat some olive oil in a large frying pan. Fry the meatballs, turning them occasionally, until they are golden brown and cooked through. Check by cutting one in half to make sure there are no signs of any pink meat.

Meanwhile, cook the spaghetti according to the instructions on the pack.

To make the sauce, heat a separate pan over a medium heat and add some olive oil. Add the chopped onion and sauté for about 5 minutes until soft and slightly coloured. Stir in the garlic and continue to cook for a minute. Add the tins of tomatoes, red wine, dried herbs and sugar. Season with salt and pepper and increase the heat under the pan.

Allow to simmer for 20 minutes, stirring occasionally, adding the meatballs to the sauce for the last 5 minutes of cooking. Remove from the heat and add the cooked spaghetti to the sauce and meatballs. Combine well.

Serve on a large platter for everyone to help themselves, or divide the spaghetti, sauce & meatballs between four bowls. Serve with some grated parmesan and crusty bread.

Serves 4

I had pondered upon whether or not I would include a Bolognese or ragu recipe in the book. It's something that most people make pretty well themselves as an everyday family meal, so is there really a need for another recipe? I thought not, that is until I made this particular recipe for a bunch of my boy's friends and then two of the parents came looking for the recipe, as it had been declared as the 'Best Ever Bolognese'. There is no need to think that I'm really fooling myself, as I know that children can be fairly whimsical with their 'best ever' statements. However, happy campers who enjoy my food make me particularly happy. This was enough to boost my ego, so I thought maybe it had earned its place in the book.

A Bolognese sauce can be made nice and quick, but when left to simmer on a low heat for a couple of hours, a much richer, thicker and tastier sauce will be the result. I normally make a double quantity of this sauce for using as the base to a lasagne the next day, or simply to have with a salad and tortilla wraps for tea.

BEST EVER BOLOGNESE

INGREDIENTS

2 tbsp olive oil

2 onions, finely chopped

2 carrots, finely diced

1 stick of celery, finely diced

1 red pepper, finely chopped

4 cloves of garlic, crushed

750g minced beef

Salt and pepper

200ml red wine

750g passata

2 tbsp ketchup

1 tsp dried mixed herbs

To Serve:

500g spaghetti

Parmesan

Crusty bread

METHOD

Place a large saucepan over a medium heat and add the olive oil. Fry the onions, carrots, celery, red pepper and garlic for 5 minutes until softened but not browned.

Add the minced beef and season with salt and pepper. Cook for about 10 minutes, stirring regularly, until the meat has lightly browned.

Add the wine and turn up the heat, then simmer for another 10 minutes.

Lower the heat, and add the passata, tomato ketchup and dried herbs. Simmer for 1½–2 hours.

Taste and season if necessary. Serve with the pasta of your choice, a large grating of parmesan and some crusty bread.

Serves 6

Coq au vin, or as translated 'chicken in wine', is one of those dishes that takes minutes to prepare and can be left in the oven to simmer for a couple of hours, or if time is an issue it can be bunged into a hot oven and be ready in 30 minutes. There are often times when I'm rushing between school runs, football practice and swimming and it's quite comforting to know that dinner will be hot out of the oven whenever we return back home. Coq au vin is quite nice with rice, but served alongside some creamy champ it makes for guaranteed comfort fuel for energetic school goers and busy chauffeurs.

COQ AU VIN

INGREDIENTS

6 skinless chicken fillets

Salt and freshly
  ground pepper

1 tbsp plain flour

1 tbsp olive oil

1 pack / 7 streaky
  rashers, chopped

500ml red / white wine

300ml chicken stock

4 carrots, in chunks

2 onions, roughly
  chopped

2 sticks of celery,
  roughly sliced

4 sprigs of thyme

1 bay leaf

To Serve:

Serve with Creamy
  Champ and
  green beans.

METHOD

Preheat the oven to 160°C / fan 140°C / Gas Mark 3.

Place the chicken fillets on a plate. Season with
salt and pepper then sprinkle over the flour.

Drizzle the olive oil into a large frying pan and place
on a medium heat. Add the chicken fillets to the pan
and fry for about 2 minutes on each side. Add the
chopped rashers and continue to fry for a minute.
Remove the chicken and rashers to a casserole dish.

Deglaze the pan with the wine and stock
and pour this into the casserole dish.

To this add the chopped vegetables, sprigs of
thyme and a bay leaf. Combine all together.

Place in the preheated oven for 2½ hours. Serve with some
Creamy Champ and a nice serving of green beans.

Serves 6

A big bowl of creamy champ, just on its own, is my quintessential comfort food. When I was a child, my mother would serve it piled high on the plate, and each potato tower would have a well of melted butter in the centre. The anticipation of who at the table would burst their butter well first was great. Okay, we were easily amused, but it was the 80s and games consoles, or even VCRs, were yet to be added to our little world, so butter wells were pretty exciting.

I love the addition of the mild onion taste from the scallions, but these can be left out for a plain mash or replaced with some herbs, wild garlic or mustard for a different twist. The well of butter isn't essential, but is still met with a little merriment from my own children.

CREAMY CHAMP

INGREDIENTS

1.5kg floury potatoes, such as Maris Piper, Roosters or Kerr's Pink, cut into even-sized chunks

80g butter

250ml of cream or milk

4 scallions / spring onions, finely sliced

Salt and freshly ground pepper

METHOD

Steam the potatoes until cooked.

Heat the butter and the cream in a large saucepan. Add the cooked potatoes into the saucepan and mash the potatoes well.

Add in the spring onions and mash using a wooden spoon until smooth and creamy.

Season to taste with salt and pepper and serve immediately.

Serves 6

The most welcoming dinner, during the harsh winter months, would have to be a robust casserole or a hearty stew. Boeuf Bourguignon is one of my favourites. It is a flavoursome stew that greatly benefits from slow cooking over a long period of time. I particularly like this dish as it can be prepared early in the day, popped into the oven and will bubble away quite happily for a few hours on a low heat. It also serves well when left in the fridge overnight only to be reheated the next day. Another great advantage of this delicious dish is that it can be made easily on a budget. A stew is one dinner that is very economical to make, as a less expensive cut of meat greatly benefits from this slower method of cooking. All of the ingredients infuse together beautifully, and the end result is a dish full of wonderful, heart-warming flavours. The perfect accompaniment for boeuf Bourguignon would be creamy mashed potatoes, but baked or boiled new potatoes would also be great. Another addition to making boeuf Bourguignon is the wonderful aroma in the kitchen while this dish is cooking; it is simply divine.

BOEUF BOURGUIGNON

INGREDIENTS

1.5 kg stewing beef, diced

2tbsp plain flour

Salt and freshly ground pepper

2tbsp olive oil / rapeseed oil

180g streaky bacon, chopped

1 onion, diced

4 garlic cloves, crushed

500g carrots, diced

1 stick of celery, diced

2tbsp tomato purée

500ml red wine

300ml beef stock, or
  1 beef stock cube in
  300ml boiling water

Bouquet garni - {2 sprigs of
  thyme, 2 bay leaves and 4
  sprigs of parsley tied together}

25g butter

250g mushrooms

METHOD

Preheat the oven to 200°C / fan 180°C / Gas Mark 6.

Toss the beef in some seasoned flour.

Heat the oil in the casserole dish and cook the beef in batches.

Heat a little more oil in the dish and add the bacon, onion and garlic. Cook for five mins until golden then add the carrots and celery. Stir in the tomato purée. Then gradually add the wine and the beef stock.

Add the cooked beef and bouquet garni to the dish. Cover and cook in the oven for 2 hours.

After this time melt the butter in a frying pan and fry the mushrooms for 5 mins. Add to the dish and return to the oven for an additional 15 mins.

Season and serve with creamy mashed potatoes.

Serves 6

To Serve:

Serve with creamy
  mashed potatoes.

I normally cook dinner in the middle of the day, as this is what suits most in the house. When it comes to evening time the children often feel like they should be having something more substantial than just a toastie. As much as I like to cook, I often don't feel like taking out a load of saucepans to start into more cooking when the kitchen has just been cleaned. So, out of a need to fill hungry tummies, while not using too many appliances, this dish was developed.

I use ingredients that I would normally have in the press and fridge, but these are easily altered. I love the combination of feta with the parmesan, but feel free to use a nice cheddar in its place, while sun-dried tomato pesto can also be used in place of the basil pesto. This is a quick and very tasty tea, which will create very little washing up.

CHEESY PESTO PASTA

INGREDIENTS

300g spaghetti

3tbsp basil pesto

50g parmesan cheese{plus a little extra for serving}

80g feta cheese

100g sun-blushed tomatoes, chopped

100g black or green olives

Freshly ground pepper

50g pine nuts, toasted

METHOD

Cook the spaghetti according to the instructions on the pack.

Drain the spaghetti, leaving a few tbsp of the cooking water in the saucepan. Return the spaghetti to the saucepan.

On a low heat add the pesto, grate in the parmesan and crumble in the feta. Stir well to combine.

Take the saucepan off the heat and stir in the tomatoes and olives. Season with a few grinds of black pepper.

Divide into serving bowls. Sprinkle with the toasted pine nuts and top with a little grated parmesan. If you have some garlic bread, serve it on the side.

Serves 4

One childhood dinner that I fondly remember is mouth-watering moist roast pork, with a rather large helping of sweet apple sauce along with a few crispy roasties on the side. I rarely roast pork these days, but on occasion I will pick up some for a stir-fry or possibly a few chops for a quick dinner. This creamy sauce with mustard and sage would be delightful served with any white meat, but works particularly well with the pork, especially when accompanying some caramelised apple slices. Basing it on the classic pork & apple combination this has a nostalgic feel but with a modern twist. The creamy sauce dolloped over some mashed potatoes is heavenly, but for a quick, 30-minute, mid-week supper, serving it with some boiled rice will make an equally scrumptious dinner.

PAN-FRIED PORK IN A CREAMY MUSTARD & SAGE SAUCE WITH CARAMELISED APPLES

INGREDIENTS

1 tbsp oil

Knob of butter

1 apple, cut into slices

600g pork fillet, cut into strips

1 onion, finely diced

100g mushrooms, sliced

Salt and Freshly ground pepper

200ml cider

200ml chicken stock, if using a cube just ½ will do

1 tsp wholegrain mustard

100g crème fraiche

10g (large handful) sage leaves, chopped

To Serve:

Serve with creamy mash or boiled rice.

METHOD

In a large frying pan, heat the olive oil and butter. Add the apple slices and fry on each side for about 2 minutes. Remove to a plate.

Add the strips of pork fillet to the frying pan and cook on a high heat until the meat is browned and cooked through.

Add the onion and mushrooms. Season with salt and pepper. Cook for 2 minutes, continuing to stir well.

Pour in the cider and chicken stock and add the mustard. Simmer for 10 minutes.

Stir in the crème fraiche, sage and cooked apple slices. Heat through for 5 minutes and serve straight away with creamy mash or boiled rice.

Serves 4

Fish and chips can be a real treat, yet I find that, as tasty as they are when tucking into them, the feeling of fullness and the stodginess from their grease can often leave me sorry for not choosing something different for tea. This version, however, has all the taste with a lot less grease and only a fraction of the calories. A proper beer batter is scrumptious on fish, and is something that needs to be sealed in oil to obtain its trademark crispiness. These goujons can be cooked in a deep fat fryer and would be perfectly delicious, but for a slightly healthier version I have sealed them in a pan with some oil and finished them in the oven. I have also found that serving fish in this way has been a nice introduction for the less-than-enthusiastic fish eaters in the family.

BEER-BATTERED FISH GOUJONS WITH MUSHY PEAS

INGREDIENTS

Mushy Peas:

200g peas, steamed

1 tbsp crème fraiche

4/5 mint leaves, chopped

Salt & freshly ground pepper

Fish Goujons:

500g hake, cod or pollock, boned and cut into strips

Salt and freshly ground pepper

225g plain flour, plus extra for dusting

3tsp baking powder

300ml beer

3tbsp sunflower oil

METHOD

First, prepare the mushy peas. Add the peas, crème fraiche and mint leaves to a food processor and blitz for a few seconds, leaving some of the peas simply crushed. Taste and season with a little salt and pepper. Transfer to a bowl. Cover and keep them warm until the fish is ready.

Place the fish strips on a plate and season each side with a little salt and pepper and a dusting of flour.

In a large bowl, combine the flour with the baking powder. Slowly add the beer while whisking continuously. It should be the consistency of softly whipped cream.

Add the sunflower oil to a large frying pan and place on a medium heat.

Preheat the oven to 200°C / fan 180°C / Gas Mark 6.

Dip each fish strip into the batter. Let any excess batter drip off, then carefully lower each fish goujon onto the pan. It will take two batches for this amount of fish.

Cook for 2 minutes on each side, or until the batter is slightly golden and crisp.

Transfer to a rack on a baking tray, and place in the preheated oven for 10 minutes, until the fish is completely cooked through.

Blot the goujons with some kitchen paper and serve immediately with oven-baked potato wedges and the mushy peas.

Serves 4

This is one of those dishes that are so quick and effortless to prepare, yet they result in a dinner so tasty that all in the family enjoy it. This is one of my preferred methods of cooking sausages. I often find that when sausages are grilled, especially the cocktail variety, the skin can become somewhat thickened, with very little meat remaining within it. I prefer to poach sausages, yet they can look anything but appealing if not served in disguise, for example encased in some puff pastry for a quick and easy sausage roll. In this recipe the sausages are essentially poached, and they benefit greatly from simmering in the tomato sauce, which becomes thick and flavoursome while it cooks. As tempting as it may be to lick the plate after gobbling down this dish, I like to serve it with lots of crusty bread, which aids in the mopping up of all those mouth-watering juices.

BAKED SAUSAGES WITH A SPICY TOMATO SAUCE

INGREDIENTS

600g tomatoes, a
  mixture of sizes

4 cloves of garlic,
  peeled & grated

12 good-quality sausages

1tsp of smoked paprika

Good pinch of dried
  chilli flakes

1tbsp balsamic vinegar

1tbsp olive oil

Salt and freshly
  ground pepper

To Serve:

300g dried pasta

Parmesan cheese

A handful of fresh
  basil leaves

Crusty bread

METHOD

Preheat the oven to 200°C / fan 180°C / Gas Mark 6.

Chop the large tomatoes into quarters and leave the cherry tomatoes whole. In a large roasting tin add the tomatoes, garlic and sausages. Sprinkle over the smoked paprika and chilli flakes. Drizzle over the balsamic vinegar and olive oil and season with a little salt and a few twists of black pepper.

Combine all the ingredients well and position the sausages on top of the tomato mix.

Place in the preheated oven and cook for 25 minutes. After this time take out the tray and give the contents a good mix, squashing a few of the cherry tomatoes.

Place back into the oven for a further 15 minutes and cook the pasta, according to the pack's instructions.

Take the sausages out of the roasting tin and add the cooked pasta. Toss through until well coated. Serve the pasta and sauce on warmed plates topped with the sausages, a grating of parmesan and a few fresh basil leaves, alongside some crusty bread.

Serves 4

In Ireland we are privileged to have meat that is almost incomparable to the rest of the world. Fresh green pastures, to which our animals have pretty much unlimited access, encourage the high quality of the resulting meat. We have dedicated farmers who care well for their animals and fantastic butchers on our doorsteps who provide us with the best of cuts. Some cuts that are most suitable for a dish may not always be the most expensive. Shin beef is very affordable and works perfectly in a stew or curry. A nice little bit of marbling through the meat is ideal as it gives wonderful flavour to the dish.

This recipe is based on one that my sister Fiona, who's a wonderful cook and host, regularly makes for family get-togethers. If I were making this the day before, I wouldn't add the mange-tout, spinach or basil, as they will lose their crunch and vibrancy if left in the sauce over night. This curry is served best with rice and poppadoms.

THAI BEEF CURRY

INGREDIENTS

1 tbsp olive oil

900g shin beef, diced

Salt & freshly
  ground pepper

2 onions, finely chopped

3 cloves of garlic,
  crushed

2 tbsp red Thai
  curry paste

1 tin of tomatoes

2 tbsp tomato purée

1 tin of coconut milk

125g mange-tout or
  baby sweetcorn

100g spinach leaves

30g basil leaves

To Serve:

Serve with rice and
  poppadoms.

METHOD

In a large saucepan heat up the oil. Add the beef, season with salt and pepper and fry for a few minutes, sealing the beef on all sides.

To the saucepan add the onions and garlic, cooking for a minute.

Stir in the curry paste, followed by the tomatoes, tomato purée and the coconut milk. Bring to a simmer, then reduce the heat and leave to cook for an hour, stirring occasionally to ensure that the sauce is not sticking to the bottom of the saucepan.

Add the mange-tout or baby sweetcorn and simmer for 5 minutes. While it is still on the heat, stir through the spinach and basil then serve straight away with a few extra basil leaves, rice and poppadoms.

Serves 6

BAKED WITH
LOVE

The simple baking of a loaf of bread or a tray of buns can give such warmth to the soul. Baking for family and friends to enjoy is just so fulfilling. Preparing dishes to bake in the oven is a lot more relaxing, compared to the urgency that is normally associated with perhaps preparing the dinner. Then once in the oven that sweet waft of baking fills the air, and in turn prepares the taste buds for the delights that are in store. For me baking is very rewarding and has a great feel-good factor to it.

On an afternoon when I have a little time to spare, I can't think of a better way to spend my time than on baking. I'll only have the mixing bowl out of the press when at least two eager helpers have grabbed their aprons and are positioning themselves, ready to tackle whatever is planned. Many of my cherished childhood memories are ones by my mother's side rolling dough and icing buns, so it feels very satisfying to now have my own children by my side in the kitchen. I've always encouraged the children to cook alongside me. Spending time together baking or cooking is an opportunity for valued family time. It's an activity that can be enjoyed together without even leaving the house and at no extra cost.

There is a marvellous bond that can be made with other family members, and especially children, through baking and cooking together. Not only are valuable memories being created, but also baking is a fantastic activity that can be a lot of fun and equally educational. I taught cookery classes to children, from my kitchen, for two years, and found it wonderful how much the children actually learnt from each lesson. Working through a recipe encourages a child to read and teaches them how to follow directions. Even the easiest of recipes can help to develop a young child's hand–eye co-ordination and fine motor skills; mixing, sifting, stirring, rolling, chopping, snipping and sprinkling all take concentration. Using weighing scales can help a young child with number recognition, while also introducing maths concepts for the older child.

Baking and cooking with children very much encourages healthy eating habits. In my experience, a picky eater is much more likely to try foods they've helped to cook. For children, to help with the preparation of a meal gives them a real sense of where their food is coming from. When better to discuss with a child the origins of a dish or the health benefits of a particular ingredient than while working together in the kitchen? Likewise, I found that the more I cooked and baked the more I wanted to know about the food I was feeding my family. A home-made treat can often be a much healthier choice, and won't contain all the preservatives that may be part of the shop-bought variety.

For a child to produce a dish that their family or friends can enjoy is a wonderful accomplishment, which in turn can give the child a real boost of confidence. To encourage a child to cook has a wealth of benefits, but most importantly they are being taught a very important life skill. When this interest is encouraged, at an early age, it will be carried through to teenage and adult life and before long we'll all be enjoying the fruit from the seeds that we planted. The great sense of achievement when pulling a tray of buns from the oven or plating up some home-made scones isn't limited to children. I still get immense satisfaction when a recipe has turned out well and the results can then be shared and enjoyed with family and friends.

LINING TINS

Loaf Tin – Lightly grease the bottom and sides of the tin. Cut two strips of parchment paper to the width of the tin and long enough to cover the base and ends. Place into the greased tin. Lightly grease the paper. Sprinkle over some flour and then shake off any excess.

Round Tin / Square Tin – Lightly grease the bottom and sides of the tin. Place the tin on a piece of parchment paper. Using a pencil draw around the tin and cut it out. Cut a strip of paper about 2cm wider than the depth of the tin. Fold up the bottom edge by 1cm, then make cuts around the periphery about 2.5cm apart. Place the circular or square piece of parchment paper on the base of the tin, then the strip around it, with the snipped edges sitting on the base. Lightly grease the paper. Sprinkle over some flour and then shake off any excess.

Swiss-Roll Tin – Lightly grease the bottom and sides of the tin. Place the tin on a piece of parchment paper and using a pencil draw around and cut it out. Press the paper into the tin. Cut into each corner and fold down carefully.

Fruit Cakes – Extra protection is needed when baking a fruitcake, to prevent the edge of the cake overcooking. The tin must be lined as per a square tin, then the circumference of the tin needs to be surrounded with a double thick strip of brown paper, which can be secured with a string.

BAKING TIPS

❀ For a recipe to work, and where baking differs from cooking, is that ingredients must be properly weighed.

❀ Eggs and butter should be out of the fridge and at room temperature for at least an hour before using.

❀ Put on the oven before weighing out ingredients. It's important that the oven is at the correct temperature before putting in the cake / bread. When in, avoid opening and closing the door, as cold air may cause the cake / bread to sink.

❀ Sieve in the flour to incorporate air into a mixture.

❀ Avoid over-handling scones, soda breads and pastry, as this will make the finished product tough.

❀ To avoid a mixture not rising, once the liquid has been added to the dry ingredients, get the tin into the oven as quickly as possible. The rising agent starts to react once contact has been made with a liquid.

❀ For best possible results, use the recommended size of tin or dish in each recipe.

❀ Parchment paper is best to use when lining tins, as the mixture doesn't tend to stick to it. If using greaseproof paper give it a little grease after lining the tin.

❀ If you run out of muffin / bun cases, cut out squares of parchment paper to line the bun tray.

❀ To test if a cake is cooked, insert a dry skewer or cocktail stick into the centre of the cake. It should come out dry.

❀ Home-baked goods generally taste better, and this most often comes down to the quality of ingredients used. When baking, or indeed cooking, the quality of the finished dish will always reflect what ingredients have been used.

❀ If you are a novice baker it's important to note that baking isn't difficult, but practice does make perfect. So if at first you don't succeed, try and try again.

The simple soda loaf is the quickest of breads to make, as there is no need to wait for yeast to work or dough to rest. Within a couple of minutes of taking ingredients from the press a loaf will be mixed together and ready for the oven. I tend not to overwork the dough and barely knead it, but more shape it enough that it can be placed in the baking tin / tray. For this recipe I've used spelt flour, which is a great alternative to regular plain flour. It is reported that spelt flour is easier to digest, and actually some who are intolerant to common wheat are able to tolerate spelt. It's important to note, however, that spelt is not gluten-free so it is not suitable for coeliacs. Gluten-free flour and bread soda can be used in place of the spelt for a coeliac-friendly version, and for a more traditional white soda bread plain flour can be used.

SPEEDY SPELT SODA

INGREDIENTS

450g wholemeal or
    white spelt flour

1 tsp bread soda

½tsp salt

400ml buttermilk

METHOD

Preheat the oven to 220°C / fan 200°C / Gas Mark 7. For a traditional round loaf, lightly flour a baking tray, or for a rectangular loaf, grease and lightly flour a 2lb loaf tin.

Sieve the flour, bread soda and salt into a large bowl. Combine well with a fork.

Make a well in the centre of the flour and pour in the buttermilk.

Either with your hands like a claw or using a fork, mix well, bringing the dough together into a ball.

Transfer to a floured surface, dust your hands with flour and gently shape the bread into a ball. Either transfer the dough into the prepared loaf tin or place on a baking tray, and then lightly cut a cross into it.

Bake in the preheated oven for 45–50 minutes, when the bread will be risen and golden brown in colour. Tap the bottom of the bread – when it is cooked it will sound hollow. Cool on a wire rack.

Every Sunday after the dinner dishes had been washed and put away, my mother would make a batch of scones. Sunday was notoriously a day for visitors, which meant tea, baked goods and happy banter in equal measures. A few days after my mother passed away I got myself into a terrible state, as it occurred to me that I didn't have this scone recipe in my possession. I'm not sure if I was aware then, but I certainly realise now, that it wasn't this scone recipe that had me so frantically tearing through books, but more the realisation that no longer would my mother be there to give me so much more than just a scone recipe. I came to terms with not finding that recipe, and with some perseverance and lots of testing I have what I feel tastes similar to my Mam's scones. Somehow they have never tasted as good as hers did, but baked within each batch of scones are happy memories that bring me comfort. I bake these scones more than anything else.

SWEET SCONES

INGREDIENTS

450g plain flour

2tsp baking powder

50g caster sugar

100g butter, cut
   into cubes

250ml milk

1 egg, lightly beaten

For Glaze:

Egg wash – some beaten
   egg with a little milk

25g granulated sugar

METHOD

Preheat the oven to 220°C / fan 200°C / Gas Mark 7.

Sieve all the dry ingredients together into a large mixing bowl and mix well with a wooden spoon.

Add the cubed butter to the flour mixture. Rub in the butter until it resembles breadcrumbs.

Make a well in the centre of the mixture and add the milk and egg to the dry ingredients.

Mix together with a wooden spoon, then use your hands to make a soft dough.

Turn the dough out onto a floured board. Wash and dry hands. Knead lightly – not too much as the scones would become tough. Roll out the dough and cut out using a medium circular cutter, making about 14 scones.

Brush the tops with the egg wash and then dip each one into the granulated sugar.

Bake in the oven for 12–15 minutes, until golden brown. Remove and cool on a wire tray. Serve warm or cold with the jam of your choice and a dollop of freshly whipped cream.

Makes 14

I make scones every few days and sometimes I like to vary the recipe. These scones are one of my favourite variations, and are particularly good with an apple jelly jam and freshly whipped cream.

BROWN SUGAR & CINNAMON SCONES

INGREDIENTS

450g plain flour

2tsp baking powder

½tsp cinnamon

50g soft brown sugar

100g cold butter

250ml milk

1 egg, lightly beaten

For Glaze:

Egg wash – some beaten egg with a little milk

25g Demerara sugar and ¼tsp cinnamon, mixed together in a bowl

METHOD

Preheat the oven to 220°C / fan 200°C / Gas Mark 7.

Sieve all the dry ingredients together into a large mixing bowl and mix well with a wooden spoon.

Add the cubed butter to the flour mixture. Rub in the butter until it resembles breadcrumbs.

Make a well in the centre of the mixture and add the milk and egg to the dry ingredients.

Mix together with a wooden spoon, then use your hands to make a soft dough.

Turn the dough out onto a floured board. Wash and dry hands. Knead lightly – not too much as the scones would become tough. Roll out the dough and cut out using a medium circular cutter, making about 14 scones.

Brush the tops with the egg wash and then dip each one into the brown sugar and cinnamon mixture.

Bake in the oven for 12–15 mins until golden brown. Remove and cool on a wire tray. Serve warm or cold with a jam of your choice.

Makes 14

LIZ'S RHUBARB & STRAWBERRY TART

Pastry and I have only become better acquainted in the past couple of years. The negative press pastry receives, along with a little impatience on my part, could possibly have been what had me feeling defeated each time I attempted a pie or tart. It does take a little practice to perfect, but I'm glad to report that I have now conquered my pastry making fear, and the lady I have to thank for this is my mother-in-law Liz. This lady could certainly be crowned "The Queen of Tarts", as never have I seen one lady so effortlessly produce consistently flawless tarts and pies. Luckily for me Liz took me under her wing and gave me some tips and lots of advice on perfecting pastry, and really what it takes is practice. Even though I wouldn't claim to have completely mastered pastry making, I at least feel confident enough to make a tart, every so often.

My favourite combination for a fruit tart would have to be rhubarb and strawberries. The tart rhubarb marries marvellously with the sweet strawberries, resulting in a perfectly balanced fruit filling for the biscuit-like pastry in which it is encased. The rhubarb will produce quite a bit of juice, so a tablespoon of cornflour will help to thicken the syrup as the tart is cooking. I still place a tray on the bottom rack under the tart as it cooks, just in case any of the sugary syrup oozes out. The quantity in this recipe is for two tarts, so one for now and one as an 'emergency tart' for the freezer. Any type of fruit tart or pie freezes beautifully, and with a few minutes added to its cooking time, the frozen tart will cook perfectly.

LIZ'S RHUBARB & STRAWBERRY TART

INGREDIENTS

Pastry

450g plain flour

25g icing sugar

225g cold butter

2tbsp cold water

Filling

900g rhubarb

225g strawberries, sliced

1tbsp cornflour

300g caster sugar

Egg wash – *made with one beaten egg and a dash of milk*

To Serve:

Soft brown sugar

Softly whipped cream

METHOD

Preheat the oven to 200°C / fan 180°C / Gas Mark 6.

First, make the pastry. Sieve the flour and the icing sugar into a bowl. Rub in the butter then gradually add the water and bring the pastry together in a ball. Turn out onto a piece of floured greaseproof paper, flatten into a round wrap and chill. This pastry needs to be chilled for at least an hour.

Divide the pastry in two. To make the tarts, roll out the pastry 1/8 inch (3mm) thick approximately, and use about 2/3 of each ball to line the tart tins. Divide the sliced rhubarb and strawberries between the two tarts, sprinkle over the cornflour and the caster sugar.

Roll out the remaining two balls of pastry to make a lid. Place over the fruit and seal the edges. Score a few times with a fork to allow the steam to escape while the tart is baking. Brush with the egg wash.

Bake in the preheated oven for approx. 45 minutes, until golden brown. Serve with a little sprinkling of soft brown sugar and a dollop of softly whipped cream.

Makes 2 tarts

BERNIE'S BASIC BUN MIXTURE

A plain bun is possibly one of the easiest items to bake, yet this unassuming bun can hold so many possibilities, and it can be as simple or as elaborate as you please.

No matter what it is that I am baking I will use butter, as I love the taste and the texture that it lends to whatever it's added to. This bun recipe, however, is the one exception. It is one that my mother made for many years and consequently became a true favourite of mine.

My mother held a healthy diet and was of normal weight, but family history can greatly determine what our risk factors are in life. We have a strong family history of heart disease, and my mother, who suffered from high cholesterol, was amongst those affected. On meeting with cardiologists, low-fat dairy spreads, such as Flora, were always recommended in place of butter. My mother was raised on country butter, and had a long-standing love affair with it, so this was indeed a difficult task. She still couldn't resist a glaze of buttery goodness over her potatoes or thinly spread over her freshly baked soda bread, however she did substitute the butter in her baking. As Flora Light, out of the best of intentions, was always well stocked in our fridge, this was to be her new baking fat. The buns made with the Flora Light would always be light and fluffy, so this became our ultimate family recipe for buns. If you prefer, butter of course can be used in place of the Flora.

BERNIE'S BASIC BUN MIXTURE

INGREDIENTS

225g Flora Light

225g caster sugar

1tsp vanilla extract

3 free-range eggs

280g self-raising flour, sieved

30ml milk

METHOD

Preheat the oven to 200°C / fan 180°C / Gas Mark 6.

Place the Flora, sugar and vanilla extract into a bowl and cream together until it is a pale yellow colour, which takes 5–7 minutes.

Add the eggs one at a time, with a little flour to prevent the mixture from curdling. Mix well after each addition.

Add the remaining flour and mix well. Stir in the milk. If it drops off easily in a dollop then it is ready.

Divide the mixture between the cases. Take a spoonful of mixture with a dessert spoon, and scrape into the bun case using a teaspoon. Don't fill the case to the top.

Bake in the preheated oven for 20 mins, or until golden brown in colour. Cool on a wire tray.

Makes 24 buns / 18 muffins / 1 2lb loaf / 1 26cm bundt tin

These are like little mini apple puddings and very lovely eaten as they are, or served with lashings of custard.

APPLE & CINNAMON BUNS

INGREDIENTS

1 quantity of bun mixture

1 Bramley apple, cored, peeled and finely diced

2tbsp Demerara sugar

½tsp cinnamon

METHOD

Preheat the oven to 200°C / fan 180°C / Gas Mark 6.

In a bowl combine the chopped apple with 1 tbsp of sugar and the cinnamon.

Make the buns as per the basic recipe. Then stir in the apple mixture until it is evenly distributed.

Divide the mixture between the cases. Take a spoonful of mixture with a dessert spoon and scrape it into the bun case using a teaspoon, not filling the case to the top.

Sprinkle each one with a little Demerara sugar.

Bake in the preheated oven for 20–25 mins, or until golden brown in colour. Cool on a wire tray and enjoy.

The topping for these buns is irresistibly creamy. For an extra lemon kick, when creaming the Flora / butter for the bun mixture, add the zest of one lemon.

CREAMY LEMON BUNS

INGREDIENTS

18 cooled buns {using the basic bun recipe}

30g softened butter

80g plain cream cheese

250g icing sugar, sieved

½tsp lemon essence

½tsp yellow food colouring (optional)

To decorate:

Hundreds & Thousands, or edible flowers

METHOD

Place the softened butter and cream cheese in a large bowl and blend well.

Slowly add the icing sugar and continue to blend. Add the lemon essence and blend again.

Add a tiny drop of the food colouring, if using, and stir well. Put in the fridge for about fifteen minutes.

Either spoon the frosting into the piping bag and ice, or put a large spoonful of icing on top of each bun and spread evenly.

Sprinkle with Hundreds & Thousands, or else a few edible flowers to decorate.

The yogurt in this recipe makes for a deliciously moist mixture. I love blueberries in a cake or buns, but strawberries or raspberries work equally well here. This recipe works well either divided into bun cases or made as a cake using a bundt tin.

BLUEBERRY YOGURT BUNS

INGREDIENTS

1 quantity of bun mixture

150g Greek yogurt

100g Blueberries *(fresh or frozen will do)*

For Icing:

100g cream cheese

50g butter, softened

300g icing sugar (sieved)

1tsp vanilla extract

125g fresh blueberries

Icing sugar – *for dusting*

METHOD

Preheat the oven to 200°C / fan 180°C / Gas Mark 6.

Make the buns as per the basic recipe, but omit the milk, then fold in the yogurt and blueberries

Spoon the mixture into the bun cases or prepared tin.

Bake in the oven for 20 mins, for the buns, or 35 mins for the cake, or until golden brown in colour. Cool on a wire tray.

Put the cream cheese, butter and icing sugar into a bowl and beat together until smooth and creamy. Stir in the vanilla extract. Put the icing in the fridge for 15 minutes to harden slightly. When the buns or cake has completely cooled, spread the icing over and smooth using a palette knife.

Decorate the top of the buns or cake with some fresh blueberries and dust with a little sieved icing sugar.

When I was a child, not a birthday would pass but these ever so pretty butterfly buns would be a part of the birthday buffet. Butterfly buns look impressive, but couldn't be easier to make. This vanilla buttercream is a real favourite that I use quite a bit for decorating buns, especially when pairing with fresh berries.

BUTTERFLY BUNS

INGREDIENTS

18 cooled buns *{using basic bun recipe}*

125g softened butter

250g icing sugar, sieved

1 tsp vanilla extract

20ml milk

To decorate:

Strawberry jam and a few fresh strawberries

Icing sugar – *for dusting*

METHOD

Place the softened butter in a large bowl and blend well.

Slowly add the icing sugar and continue to blend. Add the vanilla extract and milk, blend for 5 minutes until pale and fluffy.

Put in the fridge for 15 mins.

Slice the tops off each bun and fill the cavities with a little buttercream, then a dollop of jam and a quarter of a fresh strawberry. Cut each sliced top in half and arrange on top of the filling, to resemble butterfly wings. Dust lightly with icing sugar.

Tea brack, not normally a treat that a child would enjoy, was a real favourite of mine growing up. My mother rarely made it, but it was always offered when having a cup of tea at my Aunt Nan's. I suppose I was an old-fashioned type of child, and when the choice between a mineral and a cup of tea was on offer I would always choose the latter. I fondly remember enjoying lots of cups of tea at Nan's kitchen table while soaking up any bit of news being shared by the adults. Nan's kitchen is still a place most welcoming, and barely would a foot be inside her homely kitchen but a hot cup of tea would be placed in your palm and happy banter would ensue.

Nan's tea brack is the best I've ever tasted and one that I now regularly make. It's deliciously moist, and feels like a guilt-free treat due to the high quantity of fruit included. A slice of this brack, enjoyed with a strong cup of tea, can almost transport me back to that happy kitchen table and leaves me with such a cherished feeling of nostalgia.

NAN'S TEA BRACK

INGREDIENTS

225g raisins

225g sultanas

110g peel

110g cherries,
roughly chopped

240ml cold tea

175g butter, cubed

450g self-raising
flour, sieved

225g brown sugar

2tsp mixed spice

1 cooking apple,
peeled, cored and
coarsely grated

110g pecans or walnuts,
roughly chopped

1 egg, lightly beaten

METHOD

Place the raisins, sultans, peel and cherries into a large bowl and add the tea. Cover and leave to steep overnight.

The next day, preheat the oven to 180°C / fan 160°C / Gas Mark 4.

Line a 26cm / 10¼ inch tin with greaseproof paper.

In a large bowl, rub the butter into the flour. Add the sugar, mixed spice, grated apple, pecans or walnuts and beaten egg. Mix together until the ingredients are well combined.

Pour into the prepared tin and smooth the top with a knife or spatula. Bake in the preheated oven for 2 hours or until the brack is cooked through. You can check by inserting a skewer into the middle and when it comes out clean the brack is ready.

Allow to cool on a wire tray. The brack will keep well for up to 2 weeks when wrapped tightly with a layer of greaseproof paper and then a wrapping of foil.

We've had hens for over four years but only recently did we get a few ducks. As a child I had a pet drake, so my love of ducks is firmly grounded. They're such lovely creatures, which are actually quite friendly and a little more pet like than other feathered friends. The daily delivery of fresh duck eggs is the main benefit of having ducks in the back garden. If you've never baked with duck eggs before I'd urge you to give them a try. They are a little bigger than hen eggs, so I usually use two duck eggs for every three hen eggs required in a recipe. Nutritionally, duck eggs are superior to hen eggs, as even though the yolk contains more fat it has less cholesterol, and the white also boasts of a higher protein content. Duck eggs produce simply the best sponges, as when whipped their volume is much greater than that of the hen eggs, which results in the sponge rising very well, but remaining light in texture. The taste from duck eggs is also deliciously rich. A light sponge, softly whipped cream and your favourite jam makes for a very tasty afternoon treat.

DELECTABLE DUCK EGG SPONGE

INGREDIENTS

4/5 duck eggs,
    weighing approximately
    350g in their shells

175g caster sugar

175g plain flour, sieved

2tbsp raspberry jam

200ml cream, whipped

Icing sugar - *for dusting*

METHOD

Preheat the oven to 200°C / fan180°C / Gas Mark 6. Butter and flour two 8-inch sandwich tins then carefully line the base with two circles of parchment paper.

Whisk the eggs and sugar together for about 7–10 minutes until thick and fluffy.

Carefully fold in the sieved flour.

Divide the mixture between the prepared tins and bake in the preheated oven for 25 minutes, or until an inserted skewer comes out clean.

Turn the cakes out carefully onto a wire rack and leave to completely cool.

Place one cake on a plate and spread with a layer of raspberry jam. Then top with the whipped cream and place the second cake on top. Dust generously with icing sugar and serve.

Home-made cookies and large glasses of milk have seen us through many a tearful situation in our house. You may know the type I'm talking about; the ones that will be forgotten by tomorrow but are completely devastating today. I'm a big fan of making cookie dough as it can be popped into the freezer, at hand for any emergency after school tears, or to have with a cuppa for an unannounced visitor. I have many cookie recipes that I like to make, yet it took several attempts before I was truly happy with these peanut & chocolate chip cookies, but now they are a family favourite. I love the combination of smooth chocolate with salty peanuts, and in cookie form they marry deliciously together.

PEANUT & CHOCOLATE CHIP COOKIES

INGREDIENTS

175g butter, softened

115g light brown sugar

150g granulated sugar

1 free-range egg

1tsp vanilla extract

260g plain flour

1tsp baking powder

125g chocolate chips

100g peanuts, roughly chopped

METHOD

In a large mixing bowl, cream the butter and sugars together until pale and creamy.

Lightly whisk the egg in a cup and add the vanilla extract. Slowly add this to the mixing bowl, whisking all the time.

Sieve the flour and baking powder into a bowl, and then add to the mixing bowl.

Add the chocolate chips and the peanuts and beat again until they are evenly distributed.

Form the dough into a log and wrap in cling film. Refrigerate for at least half an hour before baking. The dough will also sit happily in the fridge for a couple of days, or else can be popped into the freezer at this stage.

Preheat the oven to 200°C / fan 180°C / Gas Mark 6. Line three baking trays with parchment paper.

Take the cookie dough from the fridge and cut the dough into slices of about 4 cm thick.

Bake for about 10–15 mins, or until golden. Leave to cool slightly on the tray before transferring to a wire rack.

Makes 18

A few years back, when I first made a Carrot Cake with my children, they were amazed to see how the humble carrot could be transformed into this exquisite baked treat. I always find that children have such a thirst for knowledge, and question everything, which makes the kitchen a fairly educational place to hang out. We know that carrot cake has been around for a pretty long time, but something one of the children pondered upon was who actually came up with the genius idea to use a vegetable in a cake recipe to start with. Of course with modern technology this query was easily answered. Amazingly, carrots were used in European sweet cakes since the Middle Ages, when other sweeteners were almost impossible to find, or just too expensive to buy. Beets were also found in archaic dessert recipes, as along with carrots they contain more sugar than most other vegetables. Carrots are nutritionally best eaten as a raw snack or even juiced, but are truly showcased in this rather luscious cake.

Praline is quite easy to make, and I really love the addition of it to cake frostings, but some chopped, roasted hazelnuts or walnuts could be used in its place. I've baked this recipe in two 8-inch sandwich tins, but this cake mixture would also fit into a 2lb loaf tin.

PRALINE CARROT CAKE

INGREDIENTS

Cake
250g plain flour

1tsp baking powder

2tsp ground mixed spice

250g light
muscovado sugar

250g grated carrot

4 free-range eggs

200ml sunflower /
rapeseed oil

Icing
150g cream cheese

50g butter, softened

1tsp vanilla extract

300g icing sugar (sieved)

Praline
100g caster sugar

100g almonds

METHOD

Preheat the oven to 200°C / fan 180°C / Gas Mark 6. Butter and flour two 8-inch sandwich tins, then carefully line the base with two circles of parchment paper.

First, make the praline. Prepare a baking tray lined with greaseproof paper. Place the sugar in a medium-sized saucepan and add the almonds. Place over a low heat. Do not stir, but carefully swirl the saucepan to let the sugar caramelise evenly. As soon as the mixture starts to turn to a golden caramel colour, pour onto the baking tray in an even layer. Allow to cool completely before whizzing to pieces in the food processor, or place in a bag and crush with a rolling pin. Leave to one side.

Sieve the flour, baking powder and mixed spice into a bowl, then stir in the sugar.

Add the carrots and stir well, with a wooden spoon, until they are thoroughly combined with the dry ingredients.

Add the lightly beaten eggs to a jug with the oil, then pour the eggs and oil into the bowl and stir well until all the ingredients are combined together.

Pour the mixture into the tins and smooth the top with the back of a spoon. If you want to be completely accurate with the amount that goes into both, weigh each filled tin.

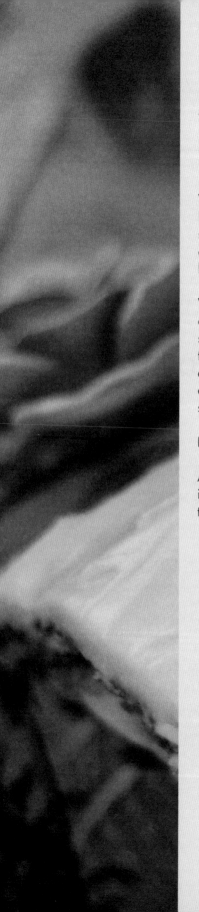

Bake the cakes, in the preheated ovens, for 25 minutes until it is risen and golden. To test if the cake is cooked insert a metal skewer into the centre of the cake. If it comes out clean the cake is ready.

Remove from the oven and leave to cool in the tins for 10 minutes before turning out onto a wire tray.

While the cake is cooling make the creamy topping. Put the cream cheese, butter, vanilla extract and icing sugar into a bowl and beat together until smooth and creamy. Place the icing in the fridge for 10 minutes to harden slightly.

When the cakes have completely cooled, slice each cake in half horizontally. Place one cake on a serving stand, and sparingly spread with cream cheese icing, then a light sprinkling of praline. Repeat this process only covering the top of the cake with the cream cheese icing and smooth using a palette knife. Ice the side of the cake with any remaining icing.

Decorate with a few pretty, edible flowers.

Any uneaten cake can be stored in the fridge. Take it out of the fridge and allow it to stand at room temperature for 15 minutes before serving.

The original Bramley Apple Tree, from which all Bramleys are grafted, still survives at 180 years old in Southwall, England. At the end of my father's garden, he has two rather large and impressively fruitful Bramley apple trees. He planted them, from seed, over forty years ago, and year on year they produce a very fruitful crop, a lot more than any of us could ever use over the autumn. I will always harvest a box of apples, in the time-honoured way that my father's mother would have used over one hundred years ago, by carefully wrapping each apple in newspaper before placing in a cool, dark area. This becomes an ever-useful stash to have at hand when an apple tart or pudding is being rustled up over the winter months.

Paying homage to the humble Bramley is easy, as many recipes with these included are firm family favourites. When faced with a bowl of Bramleys, and the choice of what to make with them, I opt for the easiest of dessert options in an apple pudding. For me, Bramley apples will always be my apple of choice when making an apple-based dessert. The tartness of the Bramley needs a little sugar to make them more palatable, but the sharpness of the somewhat stewed apples simply complements the sweetness of the buttery cake topping. This pudding can be made in a matter of minutes, and the mouth-watering scents of cakes and cinnamon will linger in the kitchen for the remainder of the day.

BRAMLEY APPLE PUDDING

INGREDIENTS

2 cooking apples

50g caster sugar

½tsp cinnamon

Cake Batter:

110g butter

110g caster sugar

175g self-raising flour

1 egg

½tsp vanilla extract

1tbsp milk

Topping:

1tbsp Demerara sugar

METHOD

Preheat the oven to 200°C / fan 180°C / Gas Mark 6. Grease a medium-sized casserole dish with a little butter.

Peel, quarter and core the apples. Cut into slices. In a bowl, combine the apple slices with the 50g of sugar and the cinnamon.

Line the bottom of the casserole dish with the apple slices.

In a food processor or mixer, add all of the batter ingredients and mix for a few minutes until well combined.

Spoon the cake batter evenly over the apple slices and smooth over with a knife. Sprinkle over the Demerara sugar.

Bake in the preheated oven for 30–35 minutes until the pudding has risen and is golden in colour. Serve hot or cold with custard, cream or vanilla ice-cream.

Serves 6

When I was growing up, shortbread was one of my favourite biscuits. Granted, there weren't too many packets of biscuits to choose from in the biscuit aisle, so shortbread would have been considered the fancier biscuit of the time. To this day I still love shortbread, not only for its crumbly butteriness, but also for how simple it is to make. When topped with creamy caramel, toasted hazelnuts and a thick layer of dark chocolate, these squares are completely irresistible. The thought of these delectable treats is enough to have my taste buds in a tizzy. They are quite calorific and oh so luscious, therefore just a little square should satisfy a sweet tooth. If preferred some pre-made caramel sauce, or dulce de leche, will work perfectly in place of the home-made caramel. As the shortbread and caramel are fairly sweet, I find a dark chocolate topping to work best, but feel free to top with a chocolate of your choice.

CARAMEL & HAZELNUT SHORTBREAD SQUARES

INGREDIENTS

Shortbread base

300g plain flour

200g butter

100g caster sugar

Hazelnut Caramel

250 g caster sugar

60ml water

150ml cream

50g butter

125g roast hazelnuts, chopped

Topping

150g dark chocolate, melted

METHOD

Preheat the oven to 200°C / fan 180°C / Gas Mark 6. Line the base of a Swiss-roll tin, 20 x 30, with some greaseproof paper.

In a large bowl, add the flour and butter. Rub together the butter into the flour until it resembles breadcrumbs. Stir in the sugar. Tip into the prepared tin and press down well with your hands to even out the mixture.

Bake in the preheated oven for 25 minutes, or until golden brown. Remove from the oven and leave to cool in the tin.

Next, make the hazelnut caramel. Place the sugar into a heavy-based frying pan or saucepan. Add the water, and stir gently to combine. Place over a medium heat until all of the sugar has dissolved. Turn up the heat, and allow the mixture to bubble, swirling the pan intermittently, until it turns a light golden colour. Watch it very carefully as the caramel can burn. Once it has taken on a light caramel colour, remove from the heat immediately.

Carefully and slowly stir in the cream and butter. Leave the sauce to cool slightly, then fold in the roast hazelnuts.

Pour the hazelnut caramel over the cooled shortbread, then top with the melted dark chocolate, smoothing with a palette knife.

Leave to set completely before cutting into squares.

Makes 15

In a bid to deliver a dense yet moist consistency to my brownies, I had difficulty perfecting this recipe. The taste was always sublime, yet it wouldn't fit in my regular brownie tin, and simply reducing the quantities doesn't always work in the scientific world of baking. I can't offer you this recipe to bake in your regular Swiss-roll tin because, alas, it will inevitably overflow. Much re-testing was done of this recipe, and I decided to eventually give in and bake it in the rather less than charming casserole dish. You see the mixture tends to rise as it cooks only to collapse in the middle just as it is ready to emerge from the oven. I could advise that, once cooled, you do as I do and transfer your brownie squares to a serving plate leaving no suspicions from your guests, or indeed family, as to how it was cooked. However, there is a rustic charm to serving a dessert in an old casserole dish.

It's important to leave a little wobble in the brownies before taking them from the oven, yet the outer crust should be nicely crisp. My children love their brownies served hot with a scoop of ice-cream and chocolate sauce, but my ideal serving suggestion is a dollop of freshly whipped cream and a few fresh berries.

CHOCOLATE BROWNIES

INGREDIENTS

225g good quality
  dark chocolate,
  minimum 60% cocoa

225g butter

25g cocoa powder,
  sieved

225g granulated sugar

3 eggs

1tsp vanilla extract

100g plain flour

1tsp baking powder

METHOD

Preheat the oven to 200°C / fan 180°C / Gas Mark 6. Grease and flour a casserole dish or a baking tray with a high edge.

In a saucepan, over a gentle heat, melt the chocolate with the butter and the cocoa powder. Stir well to avoid the chocolate burning, and once melted and well combined take from the heat.

With a mixer, whisk the sugar, eggs and vanilla extract together until pale and fluffy, which will take 5–7 minutes.

Slowly pour in the chocolate mixture and stir well to combine.

Sift the flour and baking powder into a bowl, and then fold it into the chocolate mixture.

Pour into the prepared dish or tin and cook in the oven for 18–20 minutes. Remove from the oven and cool in the dish / tin before cutting into squares and serving with a dollop of cream and some fresh berries.

Makes 15

Vanilla extract is a store cupboard must for any enthusiastic baker, as only a few drops of this sweet, comforting liquid will donate a lingering, mellow taste to cake mixtures and toppings. As vanilla extract can be expensive to buy, making your own can be a very economical move, especially if you already have a bottle of spirit left in the press since Christmas. The best place to buy the vanilla pods is online, where they are a fraction of the price you would pay in shops. This home-made vanilla extract will only take moments to make, but will keep in the press almost indefinitely.

VANILLA EXTRACT

INGREDIENTS

6 vanilla pods

400ml vodka or brandy

METHOD

Carefully split each vanilla pod lengthways then cut each in half.

Place in a sterilised jam jar or Kilner jar.

Fill to the top with either vodka of brandy.

Store in a cool, dark press for at least 6 weeks before using, and give it a shake every few days to help the vanilla to infuse.

Add a few more vanilla pods and additional alcohol when getting near the end of the jar.

I always have a large jar of vanilla sugar in my press to add to a cake mixture, home-made custard or to sprinkle over biscuits and shortbread. It couldn't be easier to prepare, and when decorated with a pretty bow and label it makes a very lovely gift for a friend at Christmas.

VANILLA SUGAR

INGREDIENTS

500g caster sugar

1 vanilla pod

METHOD

Pour the sugar into a large, sterilised jar.

Split the vanilla pod in half and add it deep into the sugar. Write the date on the jar.

Store in a cool, dark press for at least a month before using.

Keep topped up with caster sugar, and after one year replace the vanilla pod.

This is made in the same way as the vanilla sugar, but is particularly good for sprinkling over any baked, cinnamon-based cake, such as an apple and cinnamon bun. A spoonful of cinnamon sugar also gives a festive touch to a hot chocolate or latté.

CINNAMON SUGAR

INGREDIENTS

500g caster sugar

1 cinnamon stick

METHOD

Pour the sugar into a large, sterilised jar.

Break the cinnamon stick in half and add it deep into the sugar. Write the date on the jar.

Store in a cool, dark press for at least a month before using.

Keep topped up with caster sugar, and after one year replace the cinnamon stick.

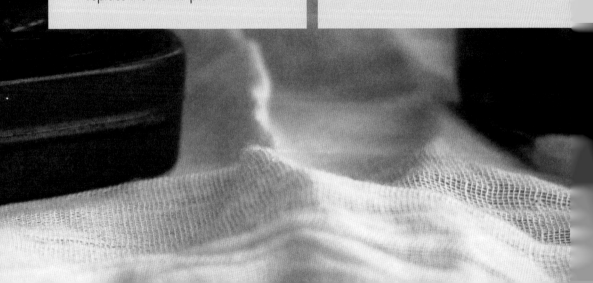

Edible flowers make a truly beautiful garnish for any sweet or savoury dish. During the summer months there is always an abundance of flowers to choose from, but naturally there are not so many throughout the winter. A wonderful way to preserve these little beauties is by crystallising them. It's very simple to do, but may be a bit too awkward for young children to manage. Delicate hands are needed, and to paint and sugar coat each one perfectly can be a little time-consuming. I actually find it quite relaxing. It's a job that I normally tackle when sitting down in the evening to watch some telly. When stored in a small, airtight container layered with greaseproof paper, these crystallised flowers should last well into the winter. These little garnishes not only look very beautiful but also taste delightful.

There are many flowers that are extremely beautiful but are in fact poisonous. Only use flowers and petals that you know to be edible and unsprayed. Avoid shop-bought flowers unless they are being sold for consumption. Wash the flowers or petals in fresh water, and dry using a tea towel, kitchen paper or salad spinner before use.

CRYSTALISED FLOWERS

INGREDIENTS

Freshly picked
  edible flowers

1 egg white

Caster sugar

METHOD

In a bowl, beat the egg white lightly with a fork.

With a clean, unused, small paintbrush, paint a thin layer of egg white onto both sides of the clean, dry petals.

Gently dip the flowers into, and then sprinkle over, the caster sugar. Carefully shake off any excess sugar.

Place the flowers in a single layer on some greaseproof paper.

Let the flowers completely dry, which could take up to 24 hrs.

Use straight away, or store in an airtight container.

Flowers & herbs suitable for crystallising include:

Chive	Lavender	Pansy
Chrysanthemum	Lemon Geranium	Primrose
Corn Flower	Lemon Verbena	Rosemary
Cowslip	Marigold Petals	Sweet Cicely
Daisy	Mint	Violas
Dandelion	Nasturtium	Violet
Elderflower		

IN THE
Family
WAY

It's often said that pregnancy is a time when a woman is at her most beautiful, blooming, glowing and boasting flawless, radiant skin. I can confirm that none of these attributes could have been used to describe me throughout any of my pregnancies. Clumsy, bloated and a blubbering mess would have been a more accurate description. I would try to reassure myself that those around me who were actually sporting the 'yummy mummy pregnant look' were likely to be already gorgeous model-like creatures in their pre-pregnancy state. However, there are many ladies who do look very beautiful while pregnant, as the bump genuinely seems to suit some, although sadly I was not one of them.

Through my years in nursing I had met many ladies who had great difficulties conceiving, as well as many who had serious complications of their pregnancies, so I'm very grateful that I had pregnancies that resulted in four healthy babies. Each of my pregnancies was very different, and no matter how awkward or bloated I appeared I was always thankful I didn't encounter any major complication. For some parts of the pregnancies I felt in complete control, but there were many times when I felt out of my depth, and so dependent on others around me. Each pregnancy was certainly very different to the last.

MY PREGNANCY DIARIES

Jack's pregnancy was the first and by far the easiest, with hardly any ailments. I went almost two weeks past term with his pregnancy and then spent 18 hours in labour. This man was comfy where he was and wasn't planning on coming out until he was good and ready. His nature is still similar to this day.

Tiarnán's pregnancy wasn't as straightforward, as I developed a heart problem called Sinus Ventricular Tachycardia, which could have been related to my extremely low ferritin levels {iron store}. It was a most frightening condition, as a few times each day my heart rate would increase to about 150 beats per minute for a number of minutes, only to slow down, and then I'd be overcome with severe nausea. Thankfully, but quite surprisingly, this completely eased when I was about 36 weeks pregnant. I always found myself to be incredibly emotional during my pregnancies. While pregnant with Tiarnán there was something that would weigh heavily on my mind. I loved Jack so much that I found it unimaginable that I could possibly have enough love to give to another child. I daren't even mention it to Diarmuid as it would have been dismissed as some pregnancy-related conundrum, but it was a genuine concern for me. Not until I held Tiarnán in my arms could I reassure myself that those unspoken thoughts were misguided. I instantly loved this little man every bit as much as I loved Jack. This taught me just how amazing the human heart can be. Before I had the children I couldn't imagine that I could feel so strongly and have enough love in my heart for four little people, as well as the people I had already grown to love in my life.

My pregnancy with Fionn was the most emotional. Not because of pregnancy- related hormones, but because my mother became increasingly unwell and passed away while I was pregnant. This easily overshadowed any ailment that came my way. In the final months of Fionn's pregnancy I mourned heavily for my mother, and cried a lot. I feared that my constant state of mournfulness would affect this little person growing inside me. But there, growing healthily in my tummy, he was my companion, he was going through this whole process with me and this gave me comfort. I was never on my own, and when he was born, he was a perfectly healthy, happy and content little man. Soon after his birth we moved into our new home, which became the start of a wonderful new chapter in our lives.

Throughout my precious Millie's pregnancy I experienced the most pregnancy-related problems of them all. It is said that some ladies find it difficult to carry a female baby, and this, in my case, seemed to be true. From severe nausea and vomiting to difficulty maintaining an average Iron {haemoglobin}, iron stores {ferritin} and Vitamin B12 level throughout the pregnancy, there wasn't a single day that I can recall where I felt well. The greatest complication came when I developed SPD {symphysis pubis dysfunction} when I was 28 weeks pregnant. This is a condition where the body produces a hormone, called relaxin, which is normally only produced when in labour. The ligaments around the pelvis then relax and in turn severe pain is experienced on mobilising. What started as pelvic pain soon developed into a real difficulty in getting about, and even to stand and weight-bear became almost impossible. As the baby grew the pain intensified, so much so that I was almost completely immobile before the birth of Millie. It was a difficult few months, but by golly has that little lady been making up for it since. She was a dream baby who slept plenty, woke on time for her feeds and in between knew how to work the crowd. An occasional burp or a windy smile had her three big brothers smitten. She had those boys hooked, and they are still dancing to her every need. She's an adorable little miss who is a sheer joy to be around. Millie was perfectly placed with the boys, and together they are just great companions for each other and for me. I feel very lucky and privileged to have these four little people in my life.

THE EARLY DAYS

The thought of childbirth can be terrifying for many women. For most it's the fear of the unknown, and this is completely natural. I always say to first-time mothers that labour and giving birth can be difficult, but you receive the biggest reward ever when the task is done. As soon as you see that baby, you instinctively want to care for him / her, and no amount of pain would stop you from having them in your life. It's a new little person, whom you've created, and the feeling of pride is enormous. I'm grateful that instantly on meeting each of my little people I completely fell in love with them and their unconditional love was clear from the start.

Even though the first few days after giving birth can be pretty hard, in terms of emotion, pain or getting into a new routine, these days are amongst my most treasured memories as a parent. Getting acquainted with this little man or woman is marvellous, and the love that radiates from parent to child and vice versa is truly tremendous. I would take full advantage of this getting-to-know-each-other stage during the early morning feeds, before the mayhem of the day would begin and while the rest of the house still slept. We can't slow down time no matter how we'd like to try. Sometimes I get a tingle down my spine when I think that I am possibly the most important and influential person in my children's lives. That's the wonderful thing about parenthood: to your children you are the most amazing person in the world. This thought often reminds me to make the most of this important honour while I still possess the title.

EATING FOR TWO

When we are pregnant there is great focus on what we're eating and how much. Throughout a pregnancy, eating the best diet possible is always advised. This healthy-eating regime, however, should really be adhered to even before becoming pregnant. Recent studies have stressed the importance of having a healthy lifestyle and diet, and of being of a healthy weight, to optimise chances of becoming pregnant.

The two most talked about nutrients that are needed during pregnancy are folic acid and iron. The benefits of folic acid are well documented, and it's advised that sexually active women should ensure that they have sufficient folic acid in their diet. The baby's spine begins to develop before a pregnancy is confirmed, and a healthy store of folic acid is important for the growing foetus.

Severe tiredness becomes part and parcel of pregnancy. In the first trimester the sheer level of tiredness is indescribable, and no amount of rest seems to make any difference. It is, however, important to rest as much as possible and listen to your body, which is trying hard to get you to slow down. Your body is going through a dramatic change, with a little person being created from a combination of cells, so it's no wonder that it's trying to conserve some of that energy. This tiredness generally eases after the pregnancy has reached 12 weeks, but if severe tiredness is still an issue it could be as a result of an Iron or Vitamin B12 deficiency, so make sure to mention this to your midwife or doctor. An optimal iron level is necessary to produce the red cells needed for a second blood supply. It's important to note that iron supplements aren't recommended before 14 weeks of pregnancy, so the easiest way to encourage a healthy iron level is through a good intake of iron-rich foods in the diet.

SOME COMPONENTS OF A HEALTHY PREGNANCY DIET:

Folic Acid – Dark leafy vegetables such as spinach and kale are rich in folic acid, as well as beans and legumes.

Iron-Rich Foods – Some of the best iron-rich foods that are recommended during pregnancy are: beef, eggs, lamb, turkey, pumpkin and sunflower seeds, spinach, firm tofu, kidney beans, chickpeas, lentils, baked potato with the skin, prune juice, leafy green vegetables and cashew nuts. Tea can hinder the absorption of iron, so it is best avoided straight after a meal.

Vitamin C – It helps with the absorption of iron. Drinking a glass of orange juice or eating fruit rich in Vitamin C, vegetables or herbs with a meal will encourage the better adsorption of iron.

Calcium – A greater intake of calcium is required during pregnancy, as the growing baby needs a significant amount to develop. This calcium will be taken from the mother's supply in her bones and needs to be replaced so as to decrease the risk of osteoporosis in later life. Five portions of calcium-rich food a day is recommended during pregnancy. Milk, cheese and yogurts are all good sources of calcium, as well as kale, bok choy, mackerel, sunflower and sesame seeds.

Vitamin D – Can accelerate the absorption of calcium in the body, so combining calcium and Vitamin D foods together, such as eggs and cheese, make for a nutrient-rich combination.

SOME FOODS TO AVOID DURING PREGNANCY {according to the FSAI}:

Liver and patés: Even though liver is a rich source of iron, pregnant women must avoid it due to its high levels of Vitamin A, which can be harmful to the unborn baby.

Softly whipped ice-cream, blue-veined or mould-ripened cheese, raw or uncooked eggs, under-cooked meat or poultry, raw or under-cooked fish, shellfish, smoked salmon, sushi: These can carry the risk of listeria food poisoning, which if contracted would be a serious health risk for the mother and baby.

Unpasteurised milk or products made from it, such as raw milk cheese. Unwashed fruit and vegetables: There is a risk of toxoplasmosis, which is an infection that could cause great harm to the unborn baby.

Shark, Marlin and Swordfish: These can contain high levels of mercury, which can harm the baby's developing nervous system, so are best avoided during pregnancy.

Peanuts: In families where there is a history of allergies, eczema and asthma, it is best to avoid eating peanuts during pregnancy as it may help prevent the baby from having these allergies.

OTHER SAFETY ISSUES:

Safe Food handling: During pregnancy it is vital to be extra vigilant as to how food is stored, prepared and cooked, all to avoid ingesting contaminated food, which can result in food poisoning and in turn be very harmful to the unborn baby.

Gardening and Cats: Toxoplasmosis is a parasite that, when contracted, can cause severe sickness. It can be mostly found in soil and cat faeces. Gloves must be worn while gardening and hands thoroughly washed afterwards. For the duration of the pregnancy it's important to delegate the job of changing the cat litter to another member of the family.

A FEW HOSPITAL BAG ESSENTIALS:

If you are attending a hospital for the birth of your baby, the hospital will provide you with a list of what to include in the hospital bag, but there are also many comprehensive guides online. I found these to be a great help when wondering what I would and wouldn't need in the hospital, and in my case to avoid landing in the maternity unit weighed down with suitcases. It's often the case that only when you are actually in the hospital will you realise there are indeed a few personal requirements you need. Here are a few of my hospital bag essentials, which may not already be on your list.

Bach's Rescue Remedy – To be used as recommended on the instructions.

Post-natal blues are very common, and most women can suffer from them. I remember becoming quite teary a couple of days after Jack's birth. It can seem unexplainable, as having this little person in your life is unbelievably incredible yet I felt unsure about even performing normal daily tasks. A midwife recommended for Diarmuid to pick up some Bach's Rescue Remedy. I had never heard of it before, as this was in 2002 and before Rescue Remedy was available in all the different forms that are available today. There were still plenty of outbursts of tears for the coming weeks, yet the Bach's remedy seemed to help. I've always had it in the press since, and subsequently used it as part of every post-pregnancy care. To cry and feel apprehensive in the early days after delivering your baby is completely normal. The body has to deal with the huge event that has occurred, and having an extra person in the home will always take getting used to, no matter how exciting it is. Always try to talk with a loved one about how you feel rather than struggling alone. If there is a possibility that it is more than the baby blues, don't hesitate to contact your midwife or doctor – they really can help.

Arnica tablets and lotion – Arnica is proven to help with post-birth bruising.

Lansinoh Cream [lanolin] – Lansinoh is a cream made from sheep's wool and helps to sooth cracked or sore nipples, especially if breastfeeding.

Witch Hazel and Gauze Squares - If stitches are in place some witch-hazel-soaked gauze can help to soothe the site.

Peppermint Tablets and Peppermint Tea – Afterbirth pains, which are the pains received when the uterus is trying to contract to its normal size, certainly increase and intensify with each additional baby. Peppermint is wonderful for soothing digestion-related problems. Peppermint tablets are available from pharmacies and health food stores. I found these tablets to be essential after my last two births, as both were caesarean sections, when it felt like every part of the digestive tract got a little tug. In turn, quite severe pains can manifest, especially while food is being digested. The peppermint is most beneficial when taken half an hour before each meal.

Hair dryer – Maybe not an essential piece to include in the hospital bag, but it's amazing how good a simple blow dry can make you feel, so for this it has earned its place for me.

BREASTFEEDING

Before having my children I had already made the decision that I wanted to try to breastfeed them. I came from a non-breastfeeding family, so before Jack's birth I attended a few La Leche League meetings, just to familiarise myself with other breastfeeding mothers. These turned out to be a massive support in the early days of breastfeeding, when I was unsure if I was doing anything right. Even with support I can clearly see why women cease breastfeeding so early. To begin with, it's not easy. No matter how tired, it's you that has to be available to this little person day and night. However, there is a lot to be said for getting comfy on the sofa and feeding the baby. As the babies grew older I very much looked forward to the genuine excuse to relax every couple of hours.

The first week is definitely quite sore time when latching on the baby. Many tears were shed, and ones that I didn't want consoling about either. During the early days for the last three babies I remember with each of them thinking that it seemed more difficult than I had remembered, however my clearest memories of breastfeeding the last child were ones of an older baby when feeding was so well established. What most ladies relate to me after they have ceased breastfeeding is the feeling of relief, but I can honestly say that after the first couple of weeks of soreness and discomfort it's by far the easier method of feeding your baby, and the benefits for both baby and mother are well researched and are found to be staggering.

Breastfeeding isn't for everyone. Some ladies experience terrible difficulties, while some simply don't want to breastfeed, and that is fine. A mother needs to be supported with whichever method of feeding they choose for their baby, and never should they be made to feel guilty about their choice. Many of us, including myself, were bottle-fed, and yes, we turned out fairly well.

POST-PREGNANCY DIET

It is essential to have a good healthy diet not only pre-pregnancy and throughout your pregnancy, but also post-pregnancy. At such a time a good intake of calories is vital, but these calories should be wholesome ones and not just from an empty source. A good diet is of paramount importance for the rebuilding of cells and to aid the body back to perfect health with the return of an optimal blood level. After suffering from such severe nausea for the term of Millie's pregnancy, my interest in food was limited to plain, uncomplicated flavours. Once Millie was born the nausea completely lifted and my love affair with food could again reignite. I was like a squirrel emerging after hibernation. I was hungry, and nothing was off the menu. I think it was the first and only time that I consciously knew that I was gaining a little weight and it didn't bother me in the slightest. I had lost a lot of weight and suffered from some muscle wastage during the pregnancy, so eating plenty of nice food and the odd swim were at the front of my post-pregnancy agenda. I could cook a meal, bake a cake or rustle up a sandwich and then thoroughly enjoy it without a trace of nausea. It was such an amazing feeling; food tasted as it should and I wanted it all. This cooking and eating frenzy was even more pronounced, as in my experience breastfeeding brought such an insatiable hunger.

It's key to remember that tiredness is inevitable after having a baby, especially in the early days when feeds every 2–4 hours are the norm. If you don't happen to have a live-in chef, which would be most welcome at such a time, or at the very least have a loved one to deliver regular meals, planning ahead of time and having a well-stocked press, fridge and freezer is a must to avoid overdosing on custard creams. The last thing you will want to do, after bringing baby home, is to pull down the recipe books, so it is always a nice idea to try out a couple of recipes at a time when you are less busy, if that is ever possible as a mother, and add some of these recipes to your repertoire. The recipes I've included in this chapter are all quick and easy. They are packed with the nutrients that are essential during and after pregnancy. These are some of the dishes that I could whip up the quickest and enjoyed the most, and I still make most of them now as part of our regular meals.

This tea is wonderful to drink as a morning cuppa any day, but is especially good when pregnant. Both ginger and mint leaves are notorious for easing the horrendous feeling of nausea, whether pregnancy related or otherwise. This drink is calming on the digestive system but also very refreshing.

GINGER & PEPPERMINT TEA

INGREDIENTS

400ml water

1 inch piece of fresh ginger

Handful of fresh mint leaves or 1 bag peppermint tea

1tsp honey

METHOD

Peel the ginger and cut into thin slices.

Add the ginger and mint to a saucepan. Pour over the boiling water. Cover and leave to infuse for 5 minutes.

Pass through a sieve and stir in a teaspoon of honey.

It seems that, during pregnancy, some of us become super sensitive to smells. Believe me, this certainly isn't always a good thing. During my last pregnancy, I was the sickest of all four. I love my morning coffee, but during my pregnancies I could barely stand even the smell of it. Even though there appears to be little aroma from a cup of tea, the scent in the air from a freshly brewed cuppa was enough to make me extremely nauseous. My options for breakfast were few and far between. I would normally start the day with some ginger & peppermint tea and then, as unusual as it may seem, this creamy, smooth drink was what I could tolerate, although not within the first hour of wakening!

Nutritionally it turned out to be a very good choice. Both oats and bananas are great sources of dietary fibre. One banana has a significant amount of the recommended daily allowance of fibre. Potassium-packed bananas are great for keeping the heart and nervous system in good condition. Oats are rich in complex carbohydrates and water-soluble fibre, which encourage a slower digestion that also stabilizes blood sugar. Add the banana and oats to some calcium-rich yogurt and milk, a drizzle of antioxidant-boosting honey and you have a very healthy and nutritionally balanced breakfast in a glass. It tastes fantastic, and actually boasts a somewhat comforting aroma.

OATS & HONEY SMOOTHIE

INGREDIENTS

1 tbsp oats

1 tsp honey

1 ripe banana, cut into chunks

2 tbsp Greek yogurt

150ml milk

A few ice cubes

METHOD

Add the oats, honey, banana, yogurt, milk and ice cubes into a tall plastic jug and blend until smooth, using a hand blender. Otherwise, put all the ingredients into a liquidiser and blend until smooth.

Enjoy straight away!

Granola and muesli have many similarities, but I enjoy the former so much more. As a child I dreaded the sight of muesli, which I would often be acquainted with at the breakfast table. Why someone would choose this raw porridge mix over toasted golden flakes of corn was beyond me. My opinion on the golden flakes may have changed somewhat, but I'm still not overly impressed by muesli, so when granola first came on my radar I naturally dismissed it. Friends had tried to convince me that there were some gorgeous granolas on the market, but any pack I stumbled upon contained some dried fruits, and other ingredients that I mostly can do without. I would quite happily eat a slice of tea brack, and love to be festive with some Christmas cake, however dried fruit is not what I need to see floating in my breakfast bowl.

With the feeling that I was missing out, I decided that I must make my own. The toasty appearance and sweeter taste than muesli is credited to the oats, seeds and nuts being toasted in the oven with a good drizzling of maple syrup. Coincidentally, I didn't add any dried fruit, so it shouldn't be surprising that I actually found it a very tasty breakfast option.

My new recipe was a winner, and now not a week goes by but I make up a batch. I found it particularly good as a snack during my last two pregnancies. During pregnancy, when the dry toast and gingernut biscuits phase has passed, it is always beneficial to have a healthy alternative to snack upon. Granola is jam packed with health-boosting oats, seeds and nuts, and also can be prepared and made in a matter of minutes. Feel free to make up your own granola combination, substituting any of the seeds and nuts for your own favourites, even dried fruit if you wish. I particularly like the depth of flavour that the maple brings to the mixture, but honey can easily be used in its place. My absolute favourite way to serve granola is alongside some yogurt, fresh berries and a little drizzle of maple syrup.

RISE & SHINE GRANOLA

INGREDIENTS

300g porridge oats

50g linseeds

50g sunflower seeds

50g sesame seeds

50g flaked almonds

50g milled linseed

25g desiccated coconut

75g nuts – hazel / brazil / pecan / walnuts, finely chopped

70g maple syrup

METHOD

Preheat the oven to 200°C / fan 180°C / Gas Mark 6.

In a large bowl, weigh out all the dry ingredients. Mix well with your hands.

Drizzle over the maple syrup and combine it through the mixture with a fork.

Pour onto a large baking tray and place in the oven for 20 minutes, taking it out of the oven every 5 minutes to give it a stir and ensure it's being evenly toasted.

Cool on the baking tray before storing in an airtight container or Kilner jar.

This soup has all the components of a well-balanced, nutritious dish, which contains many nutrients that are recommended in pregnancy. Don't find the long ingredient list off-putting, as most are just store press ingredients with the addition of some fresh herbs. Even though I'd recommend this as a nutritious pregnancy dinner, it happens to be one that I make on a regular basis, as it's a truly delicious soup. The beans and chickpeas benefit from simmering in the lightly spiced stock. The noodles add a wonderful texture, while the crispness of the fresh herbs reiterates the ethos that you are eating something healthy. I would quite happily top any savoury dish with cashews, but their salty crunch is most welcoming within the softly textured beans and noodles. Serving with a spoonful of crème fraiche and a conflicting squeeze of lime adds another dimension to the finished flavour of this nutritious soup.

NUTRITIOUS NOODLE SOUP

INGREDIENTS

1 tbsp olive oil

1 small red chilli,
  finely chopped

1 onion, diced

½tsp ground turmeric

1 tsp ground cumin

1 tsp smoked paprika

Freshly ground
  black pepper

2 litres vegetable /
  chicken stock

1 tin / 350g mixed
  beans, drained & rinsed

1 tin / 400g
  cooked chickpeas,
  drained & rinsed

200g medium
  egg noodles

125g spinach leaves,
  finely shredded

2tbsp flat parsley leaves,
  roughly chopped

To Serve:

100 ml crème fraiche

Handful of chopped
  cashews

1 lime

METHOD

Heat the oil in a large saucepan over a medium heat. Add the chilli and onion. Cook for a few minutes, until they soften. Add the turmeric, cumin, smoked paprika and a few grinds of black pepper. Stir through for about a minute.

Pour in the hot stock. Bring to a boil and add the mixed beans and chickpeas to the pot. Simmer for about 15 minutes.

Cook the noodles according to the packs instructions.

Just before you're ready to eat, add the cooked noodles to the simmering soup. Stir in the spinach and parsley. Taste and adjust the seasoning.

Serve straight away, each bowl topped with a spoonful of crème fraiche, a sprinkling of cashew nuts and a wedge of lime on the side, for squeezing over.

Serves 6

Eggs are considered a whole food. As well as boasting high levels of vitamins and minerals, they contain a significant amount of one's recommended daily allowance of iron. This dish, which I christened after a marathon read of the brilliant Dr Seuss books, is one that I adore. If breakfast in bed were on the cards then this is what I would like to be served. The spiciness of the chorizo combined with the egg in a little indulgent cream, and leafy, nutritious spinach makes for a great start to the day. This could also be enjoyed as a quick and nutritious snack, lunch or tea.

GREEN EGGS & HAM

INGREDIENTS

Knob of butter

2 thin slices of chorizo

2tsp of cream

Small handful
  spinach leaves

2 eggs

¼tsp smoked paprika

Freshly ground pepper

METHOD

Preheat the oven to 200°C / fan 180°C / Gas Mark 6. Grease the inside of two small ramekins with the butter.

In each ramekin place a slice of chorizo, followed by a teaspoon of cream and then a few spinach leaves. Crack an egg into each, then sprinkle with a dusting of paprika and a twist of black pepper.

Place on a baking tray then into the preheated oven for 6–8 minutes, or until the white is cooked through and there is still a little gooiness in the yolk.

Serve immediately with some hot buttered toast.

Serves 2

Throughout my last pregnancy, as much as I wanted to eat fish, because it's packed with beneficial nutrients, vitamins and omega-3 fats, I actually never ate even a bite. This wasn't for the want of trying – surely if I could stomach taking daily vitamin-boosting smoothies, I wouldn't find it a hard task to eat something that since childhood I have loved? My real problem started when I was only about 10 weeks pregnant. I was probably at the pinnacle of my morning sickness, with very little apart from dry toast passing my lips. Like every other house it was business as normal for 'Mammy', so dinners and all other meals still had to be made and plated up.

At around this time my father was going through a sort of detox diet because of a psoriasis type condition he had developed, and in place of meat he was advised to eat fish as regularly as possible. Surely, I thought, I would manage to cook the fish once I didn't have to eat it, but this wasn't the case. I'd barely have the fish taken from the bag before I'd have to make my way to the back door, take time to catch my breath, return to cook the fish and then back to the door repeatedly. The fish had to be cooked, and no amount of scented candles were masking that fishy smell for me, so for the remainder of my pregnancy my fish-eating days were temporarily on hold, and this actually lasted until at least a year after the birth of Millie.

Throughout my first three pregnancies I did eat fish, and it was these sort of quick and easy recipes that most appealed to me. Thankfully, I now very much enjoy fish and cook it regularly, although sometimes I still get a passing pang of nausea when it first hits the pan

SALMON PARCELS

INGREDIENTS

1 lemon

4 large sprigs fennel

4 cloves of garlic, thinly sliced

4 salmon darns

Olive oil

Salt & freshly ground pepper

METHOD

Preheat the oven to 220°C / fan 200°C / Gas Mark 7.

Zest the lemon into a bowl, then slice it thinly.

For each parcel, cut a square of tin foil, about double the size of the salmon.

Place a large sprig of fennel in the centre of each tin foil square, topped with a sliced clove of garlic and a few slices of lemon. Place the salmon on top of each, then spoon over a little lemon zest, a drizzle of olive oil, a sprinkling of sea salt and a twist of black pepper.

Fold up the sides of the tin foil and place on a baking tray into the preheated oven. Cook for 20 minutes or until the salmon is cooked through.

Serve with some green beans and baby potatoes.

Serves 4

When pregnant, our blood volume increases, and since iron is transportable through our blood we naturally need a greater intake of this ever important mineral. Considering that our bodies require significantly more iron during pregnancy, yet our calorie intake shouldn't be a lot greater than it was pre-pregnancy, it is no wonder that so many of us find it difficult to maintain an optimum level of iron throughout this period. Sometimes iron-rich beef can be slightly less appealing than whiter meats when dealing with an unpredictable digestive system. Nutrient-rich lamb is a great choice for pregnant ladies as it is rich in protein, zinc and, very importantly, iron. Vitamin C is crucial in aiding the absorption of iron from foods, so generally it is advisable to pair iron-rich foods with Vitamin-C-rich ingredients. Not only does the coriander pesto work marvellously as a sauce for the lightly spiced lamb, but also coriander is itself high in Vitamin C – a match made in iron-rich heaven.

The lamb chops are French trimmed, which is simply a rack of lamb divided into chops, but your butcher can do this for you. When pregnant, the lamb must be cooked through and never served pink, as is the case with beef.

LIGHTLY SPICED LAMB CHOP WITH CORIANDER PESTO

INGREDIENTS

1 tsp ground cumin

1 tsp ground coriander

1 tsp ground smoked paprika

½ tsp chilli powder

Salt and freshly ground pepper

9 lamb cutlets / chops, French trimmed

2 tbsp olive oil

Coriander Pesto:

20g coriander

½ a clove of garlic

15g pine nuts

80ml olive oil

20g parmesan

Salt and pepper, to taste

METHOD

In a bowl, combine all the spices together and season with a little salt and pepper. Rub the chops evenly with the spice mix

Heat the olive oil in a large frying pan over a medium heat. When hot, sear the lamb chops on both sides to colour. Reduce the heat and cook for 3 to 4 minutes on each side, depending on the thickness of the cutlets, or until the meat is cooked to your liking.

Remove from the pan and allow the chops to rest on a hot plate.

Make the pesto by whizzing the coriander, garlic, pine nuts and olive oil in a blender or food processor. Stir in the parmesan and season with salt and pepper to taste.

Serve each chop with a dollop of the pesto alongside some new potatoes or couscous.

Serves 3

I first started making this bread while I was pregnant with Millie. As I mentioned, throughout the pregnancy I was low in iron, as well as, it would seem, every other tested nutrient. I was receiving regular supplementary injections, but I also tried hard to optimise my intake of vitamins and minerals from my daily diet. I love the addition of seeds in baking, as they are rich in many beneficial vitamins and minerals and make a tasty addition to any bread. Linseed is the richest form of Omega 3 found in nature. They host very impressive health benefits that include fantastic immune-boosting properties. In this recipe I have also included some milled linseed, which can be used as part substitute for flour in any bread or cake recipe. Over the past few years this has become the bread that I make most often. I keep all of the ingredients together in the press, so it only ever takes a matter of minutes to prepare this loaf before popping it in the oven. The sunflower seeds in the bread will sometimes go slightly green after baking. Don't worry if this happens, it is merely a pH reaction between the seeds and the bread soda and doesn't detract from its deliciously wholesome flavour.

MULTI-SEED BROWN BREAD

INGREDIENTS

225g plain flour

75g wholemeal flour

50g milled linseed

1 tsp bread soda

50g sunflower seeds

25g linseeds

25g sesame seeds
   {plus a few extra for
   sprinkling on top}

300ml buttermilk

1 tbsp runny honey

METHOD

Preheat the oven to 220°C / fan 200°C / Gas Mark 7.
Grease a 2lb loaf tin with butter and sprinkle in a little flour.

Sieve all the dry ingredients into a large
bowl. Add the seeds and mix well.

Combine the buttermilk with the honey. Make a well in the
centre of the dry ingredients and pour all the milk in at once.

Using one hand, with your fingers stiff and outstretched like
a claw, stir in a full, circular movement from the centre to
the outside of the bowl. The dough should be softish, not too
wet and sticky. Sprinkle in some extra flour if needed.

When it all comes together, turn it out onto a floured
work surface. Wash and dry your hands.

Knead gently for a minute and pat the dough into shape.

Place the dough in the tin and cut a deep cross on the loaf
and prick the four corners. Sprinkle with a few extra seeds.

Bake in a preheated oven for 40 mins or until cooked.
Tap the bottom of the bread – when it is cooked
it will sound hollow. Cool on a wire rack.

HOST
with the
Most

All of life's milestones and celebrations are associated with family and friends gathering together, where food will always come centre stage. Nowadays people seem to be shying away from hosting Communions, Confirmations and Christenings in restaurants and so many more family events are now being celebrated at home.

Entertaining for family and friends should never be really stressful, yet quite often the thought of it can give a shiver to any confident home cook. These occasions are all about celebrating something special with the ones we love. They should be enjoyed not only by the attending guests, but also by the host. When hosting a celebratory meal it would be most favourable to sit down, chat and enjoy the day with everyone else, but too rarely is that the case. I have found, however, that the one fail-safe way to host a big celebration, and actually not spend all the time in the kitchen, is by having most of the food prepared prior to any guests arriving.

When choosing dishes to serve at a large get-together it's indispensable to choose ones that can be prepared the night before, or at least be made earlier in the day. It's important to keep the dishes simple and uncomplicated. Even when not entertaining I will always avoid cooking dishes that require many different bowls and saucepans, so when there are extra to cater for I try to make my dinner preparations as quick and easy as possible. In most cases guests will arrive at different times, so I generally plan to plate the main food about an hour into the celebrations. It is important to be mindful that guests are coming ready for a feast and will inevitably be hungry. Therefore it's imperative, once the first guests arrive, to have some nibbles ready to be table bound. This is a job I generally delegate to the boys and can only hope that most of these nibbles actually make it to the table. When entertaining a large crowd I normally wouldn't contemplate serving starters but instead have a few nibbles to offer before the main meal. These need not be elaborate; a few bowls of hummus, pesto and some breadsticks or crisps for dipping would suffice. Add to this some olives, cured meats, a nice cheese and a little crusty bread and you'll have a rather impressive antipasti platter. Alternatively, if a little time is on my hands I may prepare a few canapés such as my Avocado & Prawn Bruschetta or miniature servings of my Roasted Tomato, Pepper & Garlic Soup.

Many of my friends have children of similar age, so whenever entertaining is on the cards it normally consists of a rather large get-together. It's important to have some form of entertainment for the children. A little table set up with arts and crafts or even a few good movies are generally enough to have on standby. Once the children are playing contently it is so much easier for the parents to relax and enjoy the delights you've been preparing for them.

The sight of a properly set dinner table is something that brings joy to my heart. I love the use of the correct cutlery along with beautifully placed table settings, glistening glasses and crisp napkins. I find, however, that I can never become too preoccupied when setting the table for a large gathering. Almost all of my celebrations involve more than eight people, so to dress a table formally would be almost impossible. A stack of plates, cutlery and plenty of serviettes are all that is needed when guests are each plating up for themselves. A tray with plenty of glasses and jugs of diluted cordial are a must for the children, but also for those who aren't indulging in a tipple.

Entertaining or not, I very much like to have either a bunch of freshly cut flowers or a small posy of fresh herbs with which to decorate the dinner table. During the winter months some bowls of seasonal fruit and nuts can be used in place of the flowers, with candles adding a welcoming glow to the feast.

A few years ago, when I first heard about hummus, I was never that bothered about trying it, as I was certain it would be one dish that I wouldn't really care for as it can look less than appealing and the included ingredients are so plain. Then, one night at a friend's party, I reluctantly dipped a tortilla chip into some hummus, only to end up scrapping every last speck of it from the bowl. My unfounded prejudice against hummus had been instantly transformed, and from that moment on I have almost always had hummus, either a nice shop-bought variety or a home-made one, lurking somewhere in the fridge for when a bowl of crisps are in need of some company. As well as being offered as an impressively nutritious dip, hummus also makes a nice cooling accompaniment to any spicy meal.

LEMONY HUMMUS

INGREDIENTS

1 can of chickpeas,
   drained and rinsed

Juice of 1 lemon

1 garlic clove, crushed

1 tsp ground cumin

1 tbsp Greek yoghurt

1 tsp sugar

75ml olive oil

METHOD

Place all the ingredients into a mini chopper or a food processor. Blitz until smooth.

To serve, place in a bowl and drizzle with a little extra olive oil & a sprinkle of ground cumin.

This has to be my favourite of any pesto to keep to hand. It can be used as you would a basil pesto, be it through pasta or in sandwiches. This pesto is fantastic stirred through some whipped cream as a topping for a tomato-based soup, but my favourite way to serve it is with breadsticks and crudités as a very delicious dip.

SUN-DRIED TOMATO PESTO

INGREDIENTS

75g sun-dried tomatoes

1 garlic clove, crushed

25g pine nuts

Handful of basil leaves

75ml extra-virgin olive oil

pinch of salt

30g freshly grated parmesan cheese

METHOD

Whizz the tomatoes, garlic, pine nuts and basil for a few seconds in a food processor.

Add the oil and a little salt and blitz again.

Sir in the parmesan. Taste and correct the seasoning.

Store in a covered sterilised jar in the fridge for up to 10 days.

Herb- and spice-infused oils are so easy to prepare, yet can make the world of difference to food. It is also a great way to preserve the flavour of summer's herbs, which you may grow in your garden. Infused oils are wonderful when used in salad dressings, mayonnaise, marinades, drizzled over cooked meat and vegetables, mashed potatoes or simply use as a dipping sauce for breads, in place of butter. When serving as a dip, I normally pour a little into a small bowl and then top with an equal amount of balsamic vinegar.

HERB-INFUSED OILS

INGREDIENTS

Rosemary & Garlic Oil
– 2 sprigs of rosemary and 6 cloves of garlic, peeled and left whole. After 5 days, strain the oil, removing the garlic but leaving the rosemary.

Fennel Oil
– 5 large sprigs of fennel.

Basil Oil
– 15 basil leaves.

Chilli & Bay Oil – 3
small red chillies and 1 bay leaf.

Lemon & Thyme Oil –
4 sprigs of thyme and 1 large lemon. Using a sharp knife or potato peeler, carefully peel off the zest, making sure not to take any of the white pith.

METHOD

Wash and dry well your herb of choice. If I'm planning to give the oil as a gift, I sometimes sterilise an ornate-looking bottle, but otherwise I use the original olive oil bottle. Simply pour out a little oil from a bottle of extra-virgin olive oil or rapeseed oil, tuck in the herb or spice of choice, top up with a little extra oil, ensuring that the herbs are completely submerged, and then replace the lid. Leave to infuse for 2 weeks before using. If the oil contains garlic or basil, store in the fridge, otherwise keep in a cool, dark press for up to 2 months. All of these suggestions are based on a 500ml bottle of extra-virgin olive oil or rapeseed oil.

When prawns are combined with avocado they really make a fantastic, heavenly combination. Avocados are regularly referred to as a super food due to their overly impressive nutritional content. They are very satisfying eaten on their own, but also make a tasty addition to any salad. The combination of flavours and textures works particularly well in this dish. This makes a very impressive-looking sandwich if you are entertaining a few friends for lunch, but could also be served as bite-size canapés with drinks. Once all of the ingredients are to hand, it will take only a matter of minutes to assemble.

PRAWN & AVOCADO BRUSCHETTA

INGREDIENTS

1 medium crusty roll

1 tbsp olive oil

1 tsp tomato sauce

1 tbsp mayonnaise

Few sprinkles of tabasco

200g cooked prawns

1 avocado, peeled and diced

Squeeze of lemon juice

Salt and freshly ground pepper

50g mixed baby salad leaves

1 tbsp chives, finely chopped

To Garnish:

Cress leaves and chive flowers

METHOD

Heat a griddle pan. Cut the crusty roll in half and drizzle the cut side with a little olive oil. Place on the pan, cut side down, and brown gently. Remove and place on two serving plates.

In a bowl, combine the tomato sauce, mayonnaise and tabasco. Add the cooked prawns and stir together to coat well.

Add the diced avocado to another bowl. Squeeze over a little lemon juice, a sprinkle of salt and a few grinds of freshly ground pepper.

Now to assemble the sandwich. Add a thin layer of salad leaves to each toasted baguette. Top with the avocado followed by the prawn mixture. Finally sprinkle over some chopped chives, cress leaves and a few chive flowers.

Serves 2

Most vegetables or indeed fruit normally lose a certain amount of their nutrients when cooked. This would be one of the reasons why we are seeing such a rise in the raw food diet. However, cooking tomatoes significantly boosts their health benefits. Tomatoes are naturally high in lycopene, which has significant antioxidant properties. Cooking tomatoes not only increases the level of lycopene, but also makes it easier for the body to absorb. This soup may seem heavily laden with garlic, yet its taste is not overpowering, but simply subtle and sweet. Topping with the creamy basil mascarpone encourages that fresh basil flavour, which marries so well with tomatoes. This soup naturally can be served in bowls with accompanying garlic bread, but I like to serve it as a canapé, in teacups with little spoons on the side.

ROAST TOMATO & GARLIC SOUP WITH A BASIL MASCARPONE TOPPING

INGREDIENTS

850g fresh tomatoes, quartered, or 2 tins of plum tomatoes

1 red pepper, cut into chunks

10 garlic cloves, peeled & cut in half

1 red onion, roughly chopped

1 tbsp olive oil

1 tbsp balsamic vinegar

1 tsp sugar

Salt & pepper

600ml chicken / vegetable stock

A handful of basil leaves

150g Mascarpone

To Serve:

100g mascarpone

2 tbsp basil pesto

Small basil leaves

METHOD

Preheat the oven to 200°C / fan 180°C / Gas Mark 6.

Put the chopped tomatoes, the pepper chunks, garlic cloves and onion in an ovenproof dish. Drizzle with olive oil and balsamic vinegar. Sprinkle over the sugar, and season with a pinch of sea salt and some freshly ground pepper.

Wash your hands and massage all the ingredients together until the tomatoes and onion are well combined with all the other ingredients.

Roast in the oven for 20 minutes.

Meanwhile, in a large saucepan heat the stock, stir in the roasted tomato mix and add the basil. Simmer over a low heat for 10 minutes.

Blend the soup until smooth with a liquidiser or hand blender.

Return to the heat and stir through the mascarpone.

To make the topping, combine the 100g of mascarpone with the basil pesto in a bowl.

Serve the soup in a bowl or teacup with a dollop of the basil mascarpone and a few small basil leaves to garnish.

Serves 6

I love a simple salad. For most dinners, especially in the summer months, I like to serve a large bowl of salad leaves along with a few different chopped herbs from the garden. When serving a salad as a dish in itself I like to dress it up a little with some meat, cheese, fruit or nuts. This is one of my favourite salad combinations that I mostly like to make in early autumn, when the greenhouse is bursting with salad leaves and the apple trees are heavy with fruit.

AUTUMN SALAD WITH APPLE, BACON & CROUTONS

INGREDIENTS

100g ciabatta, diced

3tbsp olive oil

1 crisp eating apple

25g butter

1tsp icing sugar

200g rashers, diced

1tbsp balsamic vinegar

1tbsp golden syrup

1tsp wholegrain mustard

Sea salt & black pepper

150g mixed salad leaves

75g of your favourite
   cheese, cut into slices

METHOD

To make the Ciabatta croutons, heat 2 tablespoons of oil in the pan. When hot, add the diced bread and fry each side until golden. Remove and leave to cool.

Add the butter to the pan, then add the apple slices, dust with icing sugar, and cook until the apples are caramelised. Remove and leave to cool.

Wipe the pan clean, then heat a little more oil and fry the diced bacon until crisp. Remove, and leave to cool.

To make the dressing, whisk the vinegar together with the golden syrup and mustard in a small bowl. Season to taste.

To Serve:
Divide the salad leaves between 4 serving plates. Scatter over the croutons, caramelised apple wedges, bacon and cheese. Drizzle a little of the dressing over the top.

Serves 4

My father had large herds of sheep when I was a child, so year on year pet lambs hanging around the back doorstep were inevitable. One can get very attached to these ever-friendly creatures and I absolutely adored them, so much so that my poor father was never allowed to sell any that I had really taken a shine to. It was only at the age of nine, when seeing a large truck coming to collect the other baby lambs, did I realise the truth about their destiny. All the pleading in the world couldn't convince my father to keep them – this was his livelihood after all – so I decided to take a stand by refusing to eat lamb, but then this progressed to most other meats. It actually took a few years, but I eventually decided to put a halt to my meat ban and started to eat chicken every so often, but I actually didn't eat lamb until well into my adulthood.

My local butcher sells lamb that is always less than a year in age and is sourced within miles of his abattoir. Even though I still love the sight of little lambs in the fields, and have many fond memories of these pets, I've really come to appreciate their delicious meat for its high nutritional content, its delicate, sweet flavour and its versatility in dishes.

This aromatic lamb tagine is ideal for when you are cooking for a large crowd. It can easily be prepared the day before and left in the fridge overnight, where the flavours will only improve. The next day, reheat the tagine in a low oven when your guests have already arrived and are enjoying a welcoming drink. Sprinkle with some fresh coriander and flaked almonds, before serving alongside a large bowl of couscous.

LAMB TAGINE

INGREDIENTS

1 tsp ground cinnamon

1 tsp ground cumin

1 tsp paprika

1 tsp turmeric

½ tsp freshly ground pepper

1 kg shoulder of lamb, diced

Olive oil

2 onions, finely diced

4 cloves of garlic, crushed

Salt

500ml chicken stock

1 tin of tomatoes

1 tbsp of honey

50g raisins

To Serve:

2 tbsp fresh coriander, chopped

50g flaked almonds

METHOD

In a bowl, combine the cinnamon, cumin, paprika, turmeric and black pepper. Add the diced lamb and coat it evenly with the spice mixture. Cover and leave in the fridge for 4 hours or ideally overnight.

Preheat the oven to 180°C / 350°F / Gas Mark 4. Heat 1 tbsp olive oil in a large casserole dish and add the onions. Cook on a low heat for about 10 minutes, until the onions are soft but not coloured. Stir in the garlic and continue to cook for a minute. Remove to a plate and wipe out the casserole dish.

Season the marinated lamb with a little salt. Heat a tbsp of olive oil in the casserole dish and brown the lamb in batches, leaving each browned batch to the side.

When all the lamb is browned add it and the onions back to the casserole dish. Pour over the chicken stock, tomatoes, honey and raisins. Bring to the boil then cover with a lid and place in the preheated oven for 1½ hrs.

When ready to serve, sprinkle over the fresh coriander and almonds. Serve with a big bowl of couscous.

Serves 6

I find prawns served on a plate to look ever so elegant, especially when sparingly dressed with a creamy hollandaise sauce. This dish is rich and indulgent, which would serve perfectly as a starter course for a special dinner party. I love a creamy hollandaise sauce, especially with my poached eggs, but if I ever stumble upon some impeccably fresh prawns this would be one of my favourite ways to serve them, as a very special treat.

PRAWNS WITH A CHIVE HOLLANDAISE SAUCE

INGREDIENTS

2 egg yolks

15ml lemon juice /
  juice of half a lemon

150g butter

Salt and freshly
  ground pepper

1 tbsp finely
  chopped chives

1 tbsp olive oil

200g raw, fresh prawns

Chive flowers (optional)

To Serve:

Crusty bread

METHOD

First make the chive hollandaise sauce. In a medium-sized bowl, gently whisk the egg yolks with the lemon juice, using a hand whisk.

Heat the butter until it begins to foam, then remove from the heat and very slowly pour it into the egg mixture, a few drops at a time to ensure it binds properly.

Season with a little salt and pepper, then stir in the chopped chives. Pour a little hot water from the kettle into a small saucepan and sit the bowl over it, just to keep it warm until ready to serve.

To a hot pan, add the olive oil and swirl it around. When good and hot, add the prawns in a single layer. Cook the prawns until they turn a pink colour and start to curl a little, which will take about a minute, then repeat on the other side till they are cooked through. Remove and place on two serving plates.

Drizzle the chive hollandaise sauce over the prawns, sprinkle with a few chive flowers and serve with a big chunk of crusty bread.

Serves 2

Chilli con Carne is one of my favourite dishes to serve when catering for a crowd, as its best placed in a large bowl for guests to serve themselves. The accompanying bowls of rice, grated cheddar, sour cream, lime slices, coriander and tortilla crisps are a must, as each complement the chilli so perfectly while presenting the feel of a true feast. The chilli can easily be made and refrigerated overnight and then reheated with a little extra splash of water the next day. Without the need for additional main dishes, and with such convenient accompaniments, there will be plenty of time to relax and enjoy the get-together without spending half of the day in the kitchen.

CHILLI CON CARNE

INGREDIENTS

1 tbsp olive oil

900g lean minced beef

Salt and freshly
  ground pepper

2 onions, finely chopped

6 cloves of garlic,
  crushed

2 red peppers, sliced

1kg (1½ bottles) passata

1 red chilli, finely
  chopped

1 tsp paprika

1 tsp ground Cumin

1 tsp ground coriander

150ml water

1 x 400g tin mixed
  beans, rinsed
  and drained

METHOD

Over a medium heat, add the olive oil to a large saucepan. Add the mince, season with salt and pepper then brown the mince, which will take about 7–10 minutes. Stir regularly to prevent the mince from sticking.

Stir in the onion, garlic and peppers and cook for two minutes. Add the passata. Stir well, then add the chilli, paprika, cumin and coriander, then pour in the water.

Cover the saucepan and simmer for 1½ hours, taking care that the sauce isn't sticking to the saucepan.

After this time add the mixed beans and simmer for a further 10 mins.

Transfer to a large serving bowl, sprinkle over some coriander leaves and bring to the table with a bowl of rice, a tub of sour cream or Greek yogurt, a bowl of grated cheddar cheese, lime wedges and a packet of tortilla crisps.

Serves 6

To Serve:

Boiled basmati rice

Coriander leaves

Soured cream or
  Greek yogurt

100g Cheddar
  cheese, grated

2 limes, cut into wedges

Tortilla crisps

A few simple chicken fillets encompass a world of possibilities when it comes to potential dinners. Nowadays I would never prepare or chop meat at home, as I have a butcher who conveniently has the necessary sharp knifes to hand, and will have done in a few seconds what would take me many minutes. I am ever grateful for these saved minutes. If chicken is on the menu, I regularly ask for my fillets to be butterflied. By butterflying chicken fillets they will cook more quickly, and are perfect for simply drizzling with some olive oil and fresh herbs. In this recipe the butterflied fillet makes a marvellous blanket-like covering to the creamy mascarpone filling. The butter in which the chicken is seared adds to the finished golden glaze and naturally aids the flavour. The bite from the lightly cooked cashews gives a welcoming varied texture from the succulently stuffed chicken. What are essentially cheese-filled chicken fillets may be somewhat snubbed as a dinner party dish. However, in their defence, in most cases we are entertaining our family or closest friends, and often a familiar or unassuming approach can be rather nice when plating up for those we love.

MASCARPONE-STUFFED CHICKEN & CASHEW NUTS

INGREDIENTS

150g mascarpone

2tbsp basil pesto

4 chicken fillets, butterflied

Salt and freshly ground pepper

1tbsp olive oil

25g butter

80g salted cashew nuts

To Serve:

Potato wedges

Stir-fried peppers and onions

METHOD

Preheat the oven to 200°C / fan 180°C / Gas Mark 6.

In a bowl, combine the mascarpone with the pesto and leave to one side.

Place each chicken fillet between two pieces of cling film, and lightly pound with the flat side of a meat mallet or rolling pin.

Sprinkle each chicken fillet with a little salt and pepper and divide the basil mascarpone between the four chicken fillets, placing it in the centre of the fillet. Fold over each fillet, securing with a toothpick if necessary.

Heat the olive oil and butter in a large ovenproof pan. Add the stuffed chicken fillets and seal on all sides, turning occasionally, for about 5 minutes.

Place the pan in the oven, or if you don't have an ovenproof pan transfer the chicken to a casserole dish. Cook in the oven for 20 minutes until the chicken is cooked through.

Add the cashew nuts to the pan and return to the oven for a further 2 minutes.

Serve with some potato wedges and stir-fried vegetables.

Serves 4

A big gathering with lots of food and all the family around the table is the type of meal I most enjoy, however on occasion it can be a real treat to cook a meal exclusively for just my husband and me.

The romantic notion that this could be a regular thing is a rather wild idea, and it is more something that happens by chance, and certainly is never planned for. When children are young, there is always a real possibility of them wakening within their first hour of sleep, only then to decide that, having had their forty winks, they are not really that tired any more, making it rather difficult to coax them back to bed. The likelihood of a quiet meal with my husband hasn't increased as the children have got older either. The scent of fresh food being cooked will inevitably reach their bedrooms, drawing them back to the kitchen on the premise that they haven't eaten in ages and what an awful parent I am to cook in the family kitchen without offering food to the whole family. An offering then has to be made to avoid profuse sulking.

As I'm suggesting this dish with parents in mind, I'm assuming that you actually have children who go to bed at a particular time, and hence enjoying such a meal in peace would be a doddle. Having said that, occasionally we will sit down to a meal together at night, and this is just the sort of dish I would quickly rustle up. An accompanying bowl of salad, a nice bottle of wine and the possibility of half an hour with some music in the background that isn't Dora makes for a perfectly romantic setting, in my world at least!

TORTELLINI WITH BURNT BUTTER, SAGE & PINE NUTS

INGREDIENTS

250g pack of shop-bought Spinach & Ricotta Tortellini

25g butter

25 sage leaves

25g pine nuts

50g parmesan

Freshly ground black pepper

METHOD

Cook the tortellini according to the pack's instructions and drain, but reserve 2 tablespoons of the cooking water.

In a large frying pan, melt the butter and, once it starts to froth, add the sage leaves. Turn them once and let them crisp. Remove 8 of the sage leaves to a plate to use as the garnish.

Add the pine nuts and stir through for a few seconds before adding the cooked tortellini along with the 2 tbsp of cooking water to the pan.

Turn off the heat under the pan. Grate over 30g of the parmesan and a few good twists of black pepper. Stir well to combine.

Divide into two dishes and serve with a few of the reserved sage leaves and a little extra grating of parmesan.

Serves 2

For a real show-stopping lasagne, all the components included must be able to stand on their own. A good Bolognese sauce, or tomato-based sauce if making it vegetarian, is essential, but also a thick, creamy cheese sauce and good-quality lasagne sheets are required for creating this dish to impress. A potato-based side is most often served with a lasagne, but some sliced, cooked potatoes actually work very nicely as an extra layer, giving an Irish feel to this traditional Italian dish. I adore the use of wild garlic as an ingredient, but it is especially good here when layered among the different sauces, potatoes and pasta. Its flavour is so pungent that it infuses so much extra depth into every bite. At times when wild garlic either isn't accessible or in season, spinach will work nicely in its place. This impressively layered dish is great to make when entertaining a large crowd as one large dish will serve many.

BEEF, POTATO & WILD GARLIC LASAGNE

INGREDIENTS

1 quantity of the Best Ever Bolognese sauce

6 sheets of ready-to-use lasagne sheets

100g wild garlic or spinach leaves

100g cooked potatoes, peeled and sliced

Cheese sauce:

400ml milk

50g butter

50g plain flour

100g cheddar cheese, grated

1 tsp Dijon mustard

Freshly ground pepper

METHOD

Preheat the oven to 200°C / fan 180°C / Gas Mark 6.

To make the cheese sauce, first bring the milk to a gentle boil in a saucepan then turn off the heat. In another medium-sized saucepan, melt the butter and add the flour, stirring constantly, for about 2 minutes, until the mixture comes together and begins to froth a little.

Gradually whisk in the hot milk. Reduce the heat and, continuing to stir, heat through the sauce for 5 minutes.

Turn off the heat from under the pan. Add the grated cheese, mustard and a twist of black pepper.

Spoon half of the Bolognese mixture into the base of a large casserole dish. Top with a layer of lasagne sheets then half of the cheese sauce. Next add all of the wild garlic/spinach leaves in an even layer. On top of that, add an even layer of sliced, cooked potatoes. Then add the remaining Bolognese sauce, topped with lasagne sheets and then a final top layer of cheese sauce.

Bake in the preheated oven for 35–40 minutes until browned on top, bubbling at the side and completely cooked through.

Serves 8–10

This could quite possibly be my favourite salad. It can only be truly delicious if the tomatoes are perfectly ripe and naturally in season. It works nicely as a salad to serve alongside barbeque meats or a lasagne, but served simply with some crusty bread, grilled ciabatta or freshly baked soda makes for a totally terrific tea.

TOMATO, BASIL & FETA

INGREDIENTS

1 tbsp balsamic vinegar

1 tbsp olive oil

½ clove of garlic, crushed

Salt & freshly ground pepper

6 tomatoes, sliced

Large bunch of basil leaves

100g feta cheese

METHOD

First make the dressing by combining the balsamic vinegar and olive oil. Add the garlic and season with a little salt and pepper.

On a large plate, place a layer of the tomatoes. Season with a little salt and then a drizzle of the dressing. Sprinkle over half of the basil leaves and crumble half of the feta. Repeat with another layer of tomatoes, basil and feta, then finish with a drizzle of dressing.

Serves 4

Couscous is a very convenient ingredient to have in the press, as it can be prepared in a matter of minutes and can be served in place of rice for many recipes. A few extra ingredients can really transform a bowl of couscous, making it a very tasty salad to be served alongside grilled meats, or simply popped into a lunchbox as a healthy lunchbox snack.

ROASTED PEPPER & LEMON COUSCOUS

INGREDIENTS

225g couscous

½tsp smoked paprika

Pinch of salt

Freshly ground pepper

1tsp olive oil

350ml boiling water

½ a roasted red pepper, from a jar, finely diced

Zest of half a lemon

METHOD

In a bowl, measure out the couscous. Add the smoked paprika and season with salt and pepper. Toss together then drizzle over the olive oil Stir to combine.

Pour over the boiling water and cover the bowl with cling film. Leave to sit for 7–10 mins until the water has fully absorbed.

Stir the couscous with a fork, then add the roasted red pepper and lemon zest. Mix together and serve at room temperature or else leave in the fridge to serve cold later.

Serves 4–6

CRISPY BEEFBURGER

While I was growing up, on a Friday evening burgers were on the menu for tea without fail. As a self-proclaimed vegetarian for a number of years, I was ever dubious of our Friday evening burgers, but my mother used to reassure me that our butcher made them especially for me, completely vegetarian friendly, whereby the meat was substituted with a meal, which remarkably tasted exactly like meat. I really should have smelt a fish when these burgers were being purchased in the local butchers, but I was quite a gullible child. I happily went along eating, and I must add enjoying, these burgers each week. That was until my sister brought home a college friend who was quite a serious vegetarian. One Friday evening she arrived just in time for tea, and with my mother out of the room I let her in on what was being cooked, these wonderful meat-tasting vegetarian burgers.

Unbeknownst to me, these burgers were all part of my mother's plan to get iron into a highly charged ten-year-old. My sister's friend was quick to break it to me that these burgers were most definitely made from meat. In turn, my mother was challenged and couldn't uphold the lie, especially in front of a new family friend. My poor mother's plan to sneak me a little iron-rich meat was squashed, and not for another twelve years did I eat a burger. Now, however, I love them.

Succulent, home-made beefburgers are a great favourite of Diarmuid and the kids. I've been using the same burger mix for years, so when I wanted to vary my recipe a little I decided to see what ingredients I could substitute with others. Breadcrumbs can be useful for helping to bind a burger mix together, so I decided to try out some crushed crisps in their place and they did the trick. To add another dimension to this burger, I've added a piece of creamy Irish Camembert bruised with a little butter to the centre of each of the raw burger patties. This cheese then melts, while the burger is being cooked, adding a succulent moistness to the finished burger. This can be omitted for the non-cheese-eaters in the family. When paired with a salad and potato wedges these burgers make for a truly scrumptious dinner. However, one of my favourite times to serve these impressive burgers is when a few friends are over for a game of cards or are possibly watching a match, when only a napkin and a cold drink is needed for serving.

CRISPY BEEFBURGER

INGREDIENTS

Burger Mix

450g good-quality minced beef

35g Cheese & Onion Crisps

A few sprigs of fresh flat leaf parsley & chives

2tsp Dijon mustard

1tsp smoked paprika

1 large egg, preferably free-range or organic

Sea salt and freshly ground black pepper

Olive oil

Filling:

80g Camembert

50g butter, softened

To Serve:

4 burger baps

Ketchup

Lettuce

2 tomatoes

Fried onions

METHOD

On a plate, finely dice the camembert and mash it together with the butter. Divide this into four evenly sized pieces.

Place the minced beef in a medium-sized bowl.

Wrap the crisps in a plastic bag and smash up until fine, breaking up any big bits with your hands, and put them into the bowl with the beef.

Finely chop the parsley and chives. Add the herbs, mustard and smoked paprika to the minced beef. Crack in the egg and add a good pinch of salt and pepper. With clean hands, scrunch and mix everything up well.

Divide into four portions, then, using wet hands, shape into patties that are 2.5cm (1in) thick. Make a deep indentation in the middle of each patty and push in a piece of the cheesy butter, pushing the beef back around the mixture so that it is well sealed. Chill for at least 1 hour or up to 24 hours until ready to cook.

Preheat the oven to 200°C / fan 180°C / Gas Mark 6.

Add a little olive oil to an ovenproof pan. Add the burgers and cook on each side for 5 minutes, then place in the oven for 15mins, or until the burger is completely cooked through. When cooking burgers it's important to keep in mind that any meat that has been minced must be completely cooked through, as it can contain bacteria throughout.

To serve, toast the cut sides of the baps on the grill rack and place on warmed plates. Cover one side with a large dollop of ketchup, some lettuce, sliced tomatoes then the burger, and top with some fried onions and sandwich it all together. Enjoy!

Serves 4

This is a deliciously simple dessert that makes a very impressive pudding, and would be the perfect ending to any meal. It can be presented in a large serving bowl, but when entertaining I like to divide it between some individual wine or cocktail glasses, and let it rest in the fridge for a few hours. Before serving, I normally decorate each with a few extra berries and a sprig of mint.

CRUNCHY RASPBERRY CREAMS

INGREDIENTS

225g raspberries, fresh or frozen

100g caster sugar

150ml whipped cream

75ml Greek yogurt

4 meringue nests

150g raspberries, chopped, plus a few for decorating

Mint leaves, optional

METHOD

Place the raspberries out flat on a large dish. Evenly sprinkle over the caster sugar. Leave for an hour, or until the sugar has been well absorbed by the raspberries.

Place the fruit and sugar mixture into a liquidiser or blender and purée until smooth. Pass the puréed raspberries through a sieve to remove the seeds.

In a bowl, combine the cream with the Greek yogurt and gently fold in the raspberry purée.

Crumble the meringues into the raspberry cream and add the chopped raspberries. Gently fold all the ingredients together.

Spoon into 4 individual glasses, and either serve straight away or refrigerate for a couple of hours. Before serving, decorate with some raspberries and a sprig of mint.

This tart could be mistaken for a cheesecake, yet I wouldn't like to disappoint the cheesecake lovers out there by naming it as such. It doesn't boast the clean, silky sheen that most cheesecakes possess, and it is also a lot less sturdy. It is, however, incredibly easy to make and totally scrumptious to eat. With any biscuit base I will always pop them into the oven for 5 minutes, which allows for the base to harden slightly and prevents it from becoming a crumbling mess when cut into. This zesty, creamy tart can be made in minutes, but both looks and tastes incredibly impressive.

LEMON MASCARPONE BERRY TART

INGREDIENTS

400g digestive biscuits

Zest of 1 lemon

175g butter, melted

250g mascarpone

250ml cream, whipped

200g lemon curd

500g mixed berries

METHOD

To make the base, crush the biscuits to make crumbs, and stir in half of the lemon zest, reserving the rest for serving. Add to the melted butter and combine well. Press into a loose-bottomed tin, 26cm / 10in. Bake in a preheated oven at 200°C / fan 180°C / Gas Mark 6 for 5 minutes. Watch carefully that it doesn't burn. Remove from the oven and leave to cool completely before topping.

In a large bowl, combine the mascarpone with the whipped cream.

Pour the lemon curd over the cooled biscuit base, and top with an even layer of the creamy mascarpone mixture.

Leave in the fridge to set for a few hours or overnight. Before serving, top with the fresh berries, a little grating of lemon zest and a dusting of icing sugar.

Serves 8–10

I come from a family of talkers and storytellers, and my aunt Vera was no different. She was a great lady for the yarns, and up until the day she passed away she would whisper her tales of old. As my father's mother passed away when he was only nine, Vera, who was his eldest sister, became the cook of the house. She was extremely gifted with her hands: knitting, sewing, crocheting, gardening, cooking and baking – she excelled in it all. Growing up I was a regular assistant in Vera's kitchen. She would whip up a pavlova in minutes, and always have enough meringue left over to pop on some buns or other dainty creation such as these almond meringue slices. In her recipe notes, Vera has described the base of these slices as a biscuit pastry. It's very easy to make, and when cooked tastes remarkably like shortbread. The sticky jam, soft peaks of meringue and crunchy almonds make a wonderful combination for a tray bake.

Vera was a wealth of information where baking and cooking was involved, and whenever she was hosting an event it was extravagance all the way. Her recipe repertoire was extraordinary, and each recipe was accompanied by a story. Nowadays I would very happily sit and takes notes of these family biographies, which were all cleverly baked within a pie, however, as an ever-hungry eight-year-old, the words often bypassed me as I dreamed of delving into whatever goodies she was cooking. The stories I do remember I truly cherish.

ALMOND MERINGUE SLICES

INGREDIENTS

175g plain flour

50g caster sugar

75g butter

1 egg yolk, lightly beaten

1 tbsp milk

2 egg whites

110g caster sugar

100g apricot jam

50g flaked almonds, chopped

Line a Swiss-roll tin.

Sieve the flour and sugar into a bowl. Rub in the butter until it resembles breadcrumbs. Combine the egg yolk with the milk and add it to the mixture, bringing it together to form a ball of dough.

Flatten out the ball and wrap it in cling film, then leave it in the fridge for 30 minutes or, if in a hurry, in the freezer for 10 minutes.

Preheat the oven to 200°C / fan 180°C / Gas Mark 6.

Roll out the dough and place in the prepared Swiss-roll tin. Press down well with your hands to even out the mixture. Score a few times with a fork. Place in the oven for 15 minutes.

Using an electric mixer, whisk the egg whites with the sugar at full speed for 5 minutes until stiff peaks form.

Take the pastry base from the oven and spread over the apricot jam. Top evenly with the meringue, and sprinkle over the flaked almonds. Bake in the oven for 20–25 minutes.

Cool in the tin on a wire rack before cutting into slices.

Makes 20 slices

CHILDREN'S BIRTHDAY Party

One's birthday is really such a special day and a milestone to be celebrated with loved ones. Never is it more important than when you are a child. For the perfect celebration, careful planning is put in place many months in advance by the eager birthday boy / girl. I normally let each child decide in what way they want to spend their day. Jack is now at a stage of wanting to head somewhere nice for dinner, which is very lovely, but the rest are still at the 'pack the house with as many children as possible' stage. I actually embrace the big home birthdays, as really there are only those few short years when they will want such a hullabaloo to be made about their special day. I love to help the children to organise their birthday parties, in fact sometimes I can be more excited than them.

5
TODAY
HAPPY
Birthday
Happy
Birthday
Happy
Birthday
Sail
Away

Naturally, for me food weighs heavily in the organisation of such a celebration, but for the most part what children want is a few chicken goujons, sausages and plenty of tasty treats, and kids normally aren't bothered if these are home-made or not. There are an increasing amount of children with food allergies. Most are mild, and may not have an impact on what food is served, but it is better to check with each parent just in case.

Children love to help with the preparation of their party food, so most recipes I've included can be prepared in advance, so the birthday boy / girl won't have to spend their big day in the kitchen.

In most cases I find that children are fairly well behaved when attending birthday parties, but as the host it's vital to have all hands on deck for the three hours of the celebrating. Also, no matter what, you do not want to be stuck in the kitchen when there is a dispute going on in the hall.

The older the children become, the more friends they tend to ask to their parties. Never mind the fact that younger children have yet to make many contacts, but they actually tend to have a lot more fun in smaller groups. The length of the party is debatable, but I wouldn't tend to go over the three hours. I never go heavy on decorations, but find that the more balloons that are about the place the better. However, when I had young babies in the house I would limit them, due to the ultimate popping and the inevitable crying.

There will always be one or two children who prefer to stay out of the party games and naturally would feel awkward if there wasn't anything for them to do. A movie running in the background is great, but what's even nicer is to have some sort of an arts & crafts table. It doesn't have to have anything more than what your child already has on their shelf, such as crayons, colouring pages and some child-friendly stickers. Every child seems to love blowing and popping bubbles, and I will always have a few bought in for a party, which are especially good for the children who don't so much enjoy partaking in the party games. There are many ways to make a child's birthday party special without any cost. A few party tricks can be entertaining for both the adults and the children at the party. For one of Jack's birthdays, Diarmuid went onto YouTube and taught himself some easy-to-do magic tricks. It was a great addition to the party, and the attending eight-year-olds were well impressed.

PARTY THEMES

A home-based party shouldn't be too expensive. What is needed is time and plenty of imagination. These are some fun ideas for hosting a birthday party from home, but many of the suggestions can also be incorporated into parties at a play centre or the park. When we have an upcoming party, first off we plan a theme. I quite enjoy theatrics, so I find organising a themed party a lot of fun. It is actually a lot less complicated than the novice children's birthday party organiser would think. It definitely makes for better focus when planning the food, games and decorations. I'm not one for actually buying themed birthday ware, I'd prefer not to buy, for example, expensive themed serviettes that will most likely be used to soak up some spilled drinks. Instead, I normally put together a few bits to make the theme apparent. All birthday games and food can be incorporated into whichever birthday theme is chosen. Asking the attending children to come dressed ready for the theme can help to get everyone into the party spirit, but always have a few spare items for children who come without a costume.

Here are a few party theme ideas that are sure to thrill any birthday girl or boy.

PIRATE PARTY

The pirate theme would have to be an absolute favourite by many boys and also plenty of girls. Getting to knock to the ground peers and sentence them to death, all on the premise of a party theme – what's not for them to like! Lots of skulls & crossbones along with pirate flags will nicely set the scene. Pass the parcel is a wonderful way to distribute some important party equipment. All pirates need an eye patch, and these, along with a few sweets, could be in each parcel.

As a party activity, the children could make telescopes. For the weeks before the party save any kitchen paper rolls, cover each with plain paper and allow each child to decorate as they please. 'X marks the Spot' can be played similarly to pin the tail on the donkey. Draw a simple map on a large sheet, make an 'X' to mark the treasure, and then get each child to try and pin on an 'X', with some Blu-Tack, while blindfolded.

A simple scavenger hunt can be organised by printing out pages listing items that would be outside the house, such as a stone, leaf, etc., and then the first team back can win a prize.

My boys absolutely love tattoos, so when better to set up a little tattoo studio than at their party. Children's tattoo kits can be bought quite cheaply, but even a few packs of tattoos and a little bowl of warm water will suffice for a party tattoo parlour. For this, theme skulls and crossbows will be in big demand. Some parents can't stand the sight of these tattoos, so remember to ask their permission when they are dropping off their children. To keep with the pirate theme, I think it's almost obligatory for the mam or dad to get into the spirit and deliver a few 'shiver me timbers' when greeting guests and serving out the food.

FAIRY PARTY

The fairy theme can start with the invitations, with a sprinkling of fairy dust {glitter} and very tiny writing with miniature magnifying glasses sent along with each invite. Fairy lights lit up around the room can really set the fairy scene. Pastel-coloured tulle can be bought in a drapery store and used to decorate the birthday girl's chair and the table with a little sprinkling of confetti.

Some party games could include: 'Pin the wings on the fairy'. 'Musical flowers', played similarly to musical chairs, with a picture of a flower on each chair or cushion. A 'scavenger hunt for fairy flowers' – daisies, cowslips or whatever is growing through your grass, involves printing off a picture of each and sticking it to a card for each fairy to find. 'Pass the magical fairy parcel', played as you would pass the parcel, with a little confetti inside each layer of paper before reaching the gift. 'Fairy Says', played similar to Simon says.

Butterfly buns with a sprinkling of fairy dust {edible glitter} would be very suited to an afternoon-tea-style fairy party. Any party food in the shape of a star will also look good for a fairy theme.

I often find that the best prize for any birthday party game is a container of bubbles, but they are especially suited to the magical Fairy Party. Packs for hand making necklaces can be bought very reasonably and older children will be well capable of making these themselves. A really nice idea, that we used a few years ago, was to get each child to decorate a wooden photo frame using crayons, glitter, stickers and feathers. We then took a group photo, printed them out and each child got to bring home a lovely keepsake from the party. This in turn will suffice as the party bag filler, possibly with a few sweets or a piece of cake.

A NIGHT AT THE MOVIES PARTY

Having a movie on standby is essential for every party, but older children might enjoy a Night at the Movies theme. The attending children could come dressed as their favourite movie star – I'm thinking more Harry Potter than Rambo here. If you can get your hands on an old red carpet, that would make for a very impressive entrance. If there are younger members in the family, get them involved by greeting the guests from their cars paparazzi style, calling their names and clicking photos with a toy camera. On entering the house get them to sign their autograph in the birthday book. The food can reflect cinema food such as hot dogs – the sticky sausages with buns and ketchup would suffice, and if there are older siblings they could man a hotdog stand, serving each child their 'hotdog'. The children could be placed in groups of three and take part in a movie quiz. Make up some questions from age-appropriate films and have some pre-recorded movie music for audio questions. A piñata made in the shape of an Oscar, which could contain some party treats and the ticket for entrance to the movie, could be pre-made by the birthday boy / girl. The chosen movie can be a favourite of the birthday boy / girl, but a new release, that hopefully not too many have seen, is generally a good pick. The last hour and a half of the party can be dedicated to the chosen movie. Pull the curtains, turn the lights down low and deliver some boxes of Party Popcorn with the light from a torch.

COOKING PARTY

The cooking party can be better suited to smaller numbers, so I generally would have no more than eight children. Many party foods are suitable for children to make at a party, such as the chicken goujons or the easy peasy pizzas. Have a table set with sufficient space for each child to work at, with whatever utensils they will need. The icing of cupcakes can be incorporated into any party. A table set up with a few trays of buns, some bowls of frostings, toppings and fruit, then each child can spend time creating their own masterpieces. These can be wrapped in greaseproof paper and sent home as part of their party bag treats.

SPORTS DAY PARTY

I've a couple of lads who are sports mad, so no matter what the theme of the party a game or two of football has to be included. Having an adult as the referee and then some medals, which can be bought reasonably, for the winning team will go down a treat. If having a piñata it could be in the shape of a basketball or football. Relay races, incorporating an egg and spoon race, using wooden spoons and uncooked potatoes, are always lots of run. Children love playing three-legged races, just ensure they are racing on the grass as someone will inevitably fall over. A simple obstacle course with items to jump over, crawl under and climb over can be great fun – just don't make it too complicated as you will have to give a demonstration of how it is done before the children can get started.

The Jelly boats work well as thirst quenchers for half time at the football match, and a few proper orange segments could also be snuck in. To plan a sports party can be very much weather dependent, but if there is a chance of good weather take full advantage of it. An outdoor party is a wonderful way to have the fun of a home birthday without bringing the mess of the party indoors. Big mats can be set up for the children to have their picnic party followed by the birthday cake.

A little home-made ice-cream stand would be welcomed at any birthday party, but obviously is perfectly suited to a sunny day. An older child could man the ice-cream parlour. Have three or four varieties of ice-cream as well as some wafer fans, sprinkles, chopped fruit and chocolate flakes. Each child can queue up and pick their own favourite ice-cream combination.

Most children love the sight of chicken nuggets or chicken goujons at a birthday party. The home-made variety is a much better choice than the shop-bought alternative, as not only are you saving on all that unnecessary added oil, the option is there to choose good-quality free-range chicken. This makes these tasty chicken goujons quite a healthy party treat. If you have an enthusiastic birthday boy / girl who's helping out with the party food, they could prepare these on the morning of the party, ready for popping into the oven when their friends arrive. These goujons are crunchy on the outside while the encased chicken remains tender and moist.

CRISPY CHICKEN GOUJONS

INGREDIENTS

3 free-range
  chicken breasts

50g plain flour

1tsp smoked paprika

Salt and freshly ground
  black pepper

2 eggs

100g breadcrumbs

50g parmesan cheese
  (finely grated)

3tbsp sunflower
  oil / olive oil

METHOD

Preheat the oven to 220°C / fan 200°C / Gas Mark 7.

Cut the chicken into strips, about 5 per chicken breast.

Place the flour in the mixing bowl with the smoked paprika, a little salt and pepper.

Place the egg in another bowl and beat with a fork.

Mix the breadcrumbs and the finely grated cheese in another bowl.

Toss the goujons in the flour, then remove and shake off the excess flour.

Dip the goujons in the beaten egg. Remove from the egg, letting any extra egg drip off.

Next, toss the goujons into the breadcrumb mix. Gently shake off crumbs that don't stick.

Lay the goujons on a plate. They can be cooked at this stage, but if you have time, cover with cling film and put in the fridge for an hour.

Place the baking trays in a preheated oven for 2 mins. Remove and drizzle the base of it with the oil.

Carefully place the goujons in a single layer. Bake in the oven for 15–20mins, turning them over halfway through. When they are golden brown and completely cooked, remove from the oven and serve immediately with the creamy garlic dip or sauce of your choice.

Serves 4–5

It would be hard to contemplate throwing a children's birthday party without having a few sausages on the menu. These sausages are covered with a deliciously sweet glaze that when cooked becomes irresistibly sticky. Try to seek out good-quality sausages with at least 70% pork content. Many craft butchers now make their own sausages, but there are also some good Irish-made sausages available at supermarkets.

STICKY SAUSAGES

INGREDIENTS

700g cocktail sausages

2tbsp olive oil

2tbsp honey

1tbsp Dijon mustard

1tbsp balsamic vinegar

1tsp Worcestershire sauce

METHOD

Preheat the oven to 220°C / fan 200°C / Gas Mark 7.

Place the sausages in a single layer on a large baking tray.

Whisk together the olive oil, honey, mustard, balsamic vinegar and Worcestershire sauce in a bowl, and pour over the sausages. Turn the sausages to ensure they are fully coated.

Cook the sausages for 30 minutes, giving them a turn halfway through cooking. Serve on a large platter with lots of serviettes and cocktail sticks.

Serves 4–6

This dip is perfect for dunking chips and especially chicken goujons into, as its creamy texture complements the crunchy texture of the goujons brilliantly. However, when it is in the fridge I find it hard to resist serving a dollop of it to accompany any dish. Salad wraps, grilled meats, baked potatoes and so much more taste wonderful with this as a creamy topping.

CREAMY GARLIC DIP

INGREDIENTS

4tbsp Greek yogurt

2tbsp mayonnaise

1 clove of garlic, crushed

1tbsp chives, finely chopped

Squeeze of lemon

METHOD

In a bowl, combine all the ingredients together.

The dip will keep for one week in a sealed container in the fridge.

My children really adore pizzas, and will regularly request one when the supper cards are on the table. In recent times, whipping up a home-made one has become popular. There are many options for a ready-made base, such as French bread, pitta breads, naans or tortillas, but their ultimate favourite is this scone-based pizza. Naturally, getting the countertop covered in flour and their hands sticky will always win over the option of simply ripping a packet open. Little hands can easily handle this scone mixture, and the difference to actually making scones is that it doesn't matter so much if the dough is over handled, as this only adds to the 'rustic' look of the pizza. For the cookery-based birthday party these pizzas work out marvellously, as some of the party food is sorted along with an organised activity. The dough can be topped with either this quick-to-make tomato sauce, or a shop-bought alternative, followed by any toppings of your choice. Our favourites include lots of cheese, finely diced onions and thinly sliced tomatoes.

EASY PEASY PIZZA

INGREDIENTS

Tomato Sauce

1 tin of tomatoes

1 tsp tomato purée

1 tsp sugar

1 tsp mixed herbs
(dried / fresh)

1 clove of garlic, crushed

Pizza Dough

225g self-raising flour

½tsp salt

55g butter

100ml milk

Toppings

Mozzarella cheese,
grated mature
cheddar cheese,
sliced tomatoes,
finely diced onions.

METHOD

Put all the ingredients for the sauce into a saucepan and simmer for 10mins. Allow to cool and then blend using a hand blender / liquidizer.

Preheat the oven to 220°C / fan 200°C / Gas Mark 7.

Put the flour and salt into a mixing bowl, then rub in the butter.

When the mixture is like breadcrumbs, pour in the milk.
Stir together until you have a smooth ball of dough.

Lightly flour your work surface. Divide your dough into four balls and roll out each one using a lightly floured rolling pin.

Place the dough onto a baking tray, pinching up the edges to make a crust to stop the cheese from spilling out when melted.

Cover each pizza with a layer of the tomato sauce.

Sprinkle over the cheese and toppings of your choice. Try not to overload the pizza with toppings, as it won't cook evenly.

Bake in the oven for 10–12mins, or until the sides are golden brown and the cheese is bubbling.

Serves 4

CHOCOLATE COLA CELEBRATION CAKE

A lot of emphasis can be put on the birthday cake, but many children are normally fairly full by the time the cake makes an entrance. Ultimately they will all raise their hands for a slice of this glorious-looking creation. However, younger children especially may only eat a few bites of it, and the rest will be left to waste. I absolutely dread wasting food, and in a bid to reduce birthday cake waste I've started to serve ice cream alongside the cake. This isn't to add to the overload of sugar, but more to give the children an option of having cake or ice-cream. Some will actually still want both, which is fine. In most cases the ice-cream seems to be favoured, however I still love a birthday cake at each celebration.

Normally each of my children will have a different cake picked for each of their birthdays. Last year Tiarnán picked a Chocolate Cola cake. I'm almost certain that the title had him hooked. A chocolate cake containing something that Mammy doesn't normally buy: cola. It had to be tried. Of course I said we'd give it a go, and I based the recipe on a gluten-free chocolate cake that I normally make. I must say that I was rather impressed with the result. Even though it contains cola, there isn't a distinctive cola flavour from the cake, however what the cola does add to this cake is a sweet sort of caramel flavour, and it greatly promotes the cake's indulgently moist centre. This cake doesn't necessarily need to be iced, as some cream on the side would suffice, however the chocolate cola frosting just gives it that perfect finish. It's best to make this cake the day before the party, as the flavour improves when left overnight, then ice it generously on the morning of the party.

CHOCOLATE COLA CELEBRATION CAKE

INGREDIENTS

Cake

150ml cola

150g butter

250g chocolate, 50% cocoa solids

6 eggs

175g caster sugar

Chocolate Cola Frosting

200g icing sugar, sifted

60ml cola

100g butter, soft

75g chocolate, 35–50% cocoa solids melted

To Decorate:

Golden sprinkles or chocolate covered sweets

METHOD

Preheat the oven to 200°C / fan 180°C / Gas Mark 6. Prepare a 26cm baking tin by lightly greasing the sides and placing a disk of parchment on the base.

Place the cola, butter and chocolate into a medium-sized saucepan over a low heat. Stir continuously until the butter and chocolate has melted and combined with the cola and is smooth and silky. Remove from the heat.

Using an electric mixer and a large bowl, whisk the eggs and sugar together for 5–7 minutes until the mixture is light and foamy.

Slowly pour in the chocolate mixture and gently fold through. Pour into the prepared tin. Bake in the preheated oven for 35–40 minutes. The outside will be crisp with some moistness in the centre.

To make the frosting, sieve the icing sugar into a bowl. Put the cola, butter and chocolate into a saucepan and melt slowly, stirring well to combine. Let it cool slightly before pouring over the icing sugar and mixing together well.

Remove the cake from the oven, and leave to completely cool in its tin on a wire rack.

Once cold, take the cake from the tin and place onto a serving plate. Don't worry if the cake collapses in the centre or cracks a little. Simply coat it with the chocolate cola frosting and decorate with golden sprinkles, or a variety of favourite chocolate-covered sweets. Serve with a dollop of cream or ice-cream.

One of my favourite childhood films was the very brilliant Willy Wonka and the Chocolate Factory. The whole premise of the film is still one that I find very endearing, as it has many fantastic characters that most would have to have an opinion on. One of my favourite scenes from the film was when poor old Augustus Gloop fell into the river of chocolate. It was not because I relished in the idea that this disobedient young man was getting his comeuppance, but more in awe that he was swimming in a sea of chocolate. Imagine actually soaking in a tub of edible chocolate; completely mind blowing as a child, yet somewhat obscene now from an adult's perspective. The closest I've ever come to that chocolate river is a lot less impressive, but still decadent none the less, when a rather large chocolate fountain came into my radar at a family wedding. There is something so irresistible about the vision of chocolate flowing so invitingly. It's overly indulgent, but aren't celebrations the time for pampering oneself in such luxuries?

Mini chocolate fountains are widely available to buy, and yes, as a lover of gadgets I do have one tucked away in my store. However, because of its size it can often become lost in a group of twenty energetic chocolate-loving partygoers. I actually find that a big bowl of this velvety chocolate dip works out a treat in its place. The threading of the fruit and sweets onto the skewers is very suitable for the birthday boy / girl or their siblings to do alone. I mostly serve the dip in separate little bowls or teacups, as when faced with a large bowl of chocolate dip to share, children quite often will do everything apart from cupping the chocolate up into their hands in a bid to consume more of the chocolaty sauce than the child beside them. Yes, that is experience talking!

VELVETY CHOCOLATE DIP WITH MARSHMALLOW SKEWERS

INGREDIENTS

Chocolate Dip

125g chocolate,
   35% cocoa solids

250ml cream

1 tbsp golden syrup

Fruity Marshmallow Skewers

Blueberries

Strawberries

Clementine segments

Mini marshmallows

METHOD

Pour the chocolate, cream and golden syrup into a saucepan, and place over a very low heat. Keep stirring until the chocolate has completely melted, then take the saucepan off the heat.

Pour the sauce into a bowl and leave to cool slightly while you, or your helper, prepare the fruity marshmallow skewers.

Thread a piece of each fruit onto a skewer or cocktail stick and finish with a marshmallow. Serve alongside the chocolate sauce for a messy but very delicious party treat.

Serves 4–6

These jelly boats are without a doubt the most sought after party food at our birthday parties. Children love the novelty factor of tucking into something that looks healthy yet is a tremendous treat. Jelly has always been on the menu for our parties, but serving it in this way is not only great for the children but also great for me, as it saves on the washing up of twenty bowls and spoons. For the artistic type of partygoers, the making of the sails could be part of the party activities, when each can decorate their own sail with colours and stickers, but not glitter — unless it's edible.

JELLY BOATS

INGREDIENTS

5 large oranges

2 x 135g packets of jelly, any flavour

20 cocktail sticks with home-made paper sails

METHOD

Cut the oranges in half and carefully remove all of the flesh out of the orange, being very careful not to perforate the skin of the orange.

Make the jelly according to the instructions on the pack, but add only half of the recommended amount of water, which is approximately 250ml per packet of jelly.

Place the orange halves into a muffin tin, then pour the jelly carefully into each one, filling to the top.

Allow to cool, then place in the fridge for a few hours or until set. Place the set jelly oranges onto a cutting board and with a sharp knife cut each one in half.

Decorate each boat with a home-made paper sail.

Makes 20 boats

The boys love to enjoy big bowls of home-made popcorn on their movie nights. Anything from butter and sugar to maple syrup could be drizzled over it; each of them trying hard to come up with their own signature popcorn, and some can be rather interesting, to say the least. When challenged to get together a few treats for last year's Late Late Toy Show, this was the popcorn that Jack made, and it is the best popcorn combination yet. There is something so perfect about the amalgamation of creamy chocolate and salty popcorn, and this is what makes this party popcorn so irresistible.

JACK'S PARTY POPCORN

INGREDIENTS

50g popcorn

Handful of M&M's

Handful of Smarties

50g white chocolate

METHOD

Put the popcorn and sweets into a bowl.

Melt the chocolate in a heatproof bowl set over a saucepan of simmering water.

Pour the melted chocolate over the popcorn and sweets and stir well.

Spoon the mixture into a large container and place in a fridge for an hour. Remove from the fridge, break into chunks and enjoy.

Serves 4–6

These milkshake-style smoothies make for a lovely refreshing treat at a birthday party. I will always have berries in the freezer that I have picked from the garden throughout the summer. Then, when in season, I normally stock up with a few kilos of Irish blueberries, to store alongside my own berries in the freezer. These frozen berries will last me well into the winter, and they are extremely convenient for fruity cake mixes, and are especially good as a nutritious base for smoothies. Fresh or frozen berries can be used for this recipe.

BERRY BLISS SHAKE

INGREDIENTS

100g strawberries

100g raspberries

100g blueberries

1 banana

150g Greek yogurt

2tsp honey

600ml milk

METHOD

Place all the ingredients into a large jug and combine with a hand blender until smooth. Otherwise blend all the ingredients using a liquidiser. Enjoy straight away.

Serves 4

Banana split was my favourite dessert as a child. Even though I never considered fruit-based desserts to be the most desirable choice, I could handle half a banana when 3 scoops of ice-cream and lots of chocolate sauce were inevitably included. I'm glad to say that the banana split has passed the test of time, as my own crew are quite partial to it, and that is what brought about this recipe. This hot banoffee sundae could be described as a deconstructed banoffee pie, as all of the ingredients are included, but simply served a little differently. Naturally, the children prefer their sundae served with lashings of ice-cream, but keeping it true to its 'banoffee' name, I quite like to serve it with some softly whipped cream.

I have this dessert in the 'birthday' section as even though I wouldn't contemplate dishing it out to 20 hyper partygoers, when there is very little time for cooking and all hands on deck are normally required, I would make it as a special treat for a birthday boy or girl if we were having a smaller family birthday celebration. I quite like caramelised bananas, and when served with luscious toffee sauce and softly whipped cream it's a dessert that needn't be reserved for the children's menu, but could easily be on the cards as a dinner party dessert.

HOT BANOFFEE SUNDAE

INGREDIENTS

4 bananas, sliced

1 tbsp brown sugar

20g butter

4 tbsp caramel sauce
– shop-bought or
made using the recipe
on p.80 {omitting
the hazelnuts}

125ml cream, whipped

4 digestive biscuits

METHOD

Place the sliced bananas on a plate and sprinkle with the brown sugar.

Place a large pan over a medium heat, and add the butter. Once frothing, add the bananas and fry for 1 minute on each side.

Transfer to 4 serving plates. Drizzle with some toffee sauce. Top with a spoonful of whipped cream and crumble a digestive biscuit over each.

Serves 4

The boys and Millie absolutely adore ice-cream. There could be snow belting against the window and still, if a treat of choice is offered, in unison, they will all request ice-cream. In recent years I have tried to make them different home-made versions. These guys like to eat, and granted they would always try out any new dishes I stumble upon, but ever the honest critics that they are I just couldn't convince them that home-made was better on this one, until about a year ago, when I made this 'ice-cream' for the first time. The mixture seemed more smoothie like than ice-cream, yet when popped into the freezer for a couple of hours it hardened enough to scoop, and when placed on top of a wafer cone even the most discerning ice-cream connoisseur will have difficulties faulting it. This has become one of the children's favourite desserts, and, as it's pretty healthy, a drizzle of chocolate sauce could even be forgiven for that extra special occasion. Give it a try; I'm sure you'll love it as much as my children do!

TROPICAL YOGURT ICE-CREAM

INGREDIENTS

3 ripe bananas, peeled and chopped

2 mangos, peeled and chopped

6 rings of pineapple from a tin, or ¼ of a fresh pineapple, peeled and chopped

500g Greek yogurt

Squeeze of lemon juice

2tbsp icing sugar

METHOD

Place the chopped banana, mango and pineapple into a sealed container and freeze for 2–3 hours.

Place the frozen fruit, yogurt, lemon juice and icing sugar in a blender or food processor and blend until smooth. This is delicious eaten straight away, but to serve in an ice-cream cone, place it into a freezer-proof dish {I normally use an old ice-cream container} and place in the freezer for a couple of hours.

If freezing overnight, make sure to remove from the freezer and allow to rest at room temperature for one hour before serving.

Serves 6–8

The combination for this cake has included some of my favourite treats to snack upon. Salty peanuts, creamy chocolate, mouth-melting Maltesers, mixed together with just a few plain Marietta biscuits and Rice Krispies, which slightly balance all that lusciousness perfectly. Whether I make these into squares or a cake, I find myself forever nibbling away at them throughout a party. They are simply irresistible. In fact, they are so irresistible that I will only make them when I'm either hosting a get-together or gifting them to a friend, because if left in my press there would be no stopping me from eating the entire tray.

This mixture can be quite easily made into a party cake, as once placed in a lined container, such as a pudding bowl, it will set perfectly after a couple of hours. One year we had it as a mountain, which was perfect for army men to fight on, and we decorated the set cake with lots of army toys. Another version that my boys quite like is making it into a cannonball, which looks very appropriate at a pirate's party. A 'fuse' can be created using a cocktail stick to support a piece of twine, along with a little drawing with 'boom!' added to the front of the melted chocolate.

CHOCOLATE NUT SQUARES / CHOCOLATE NUT CANNONBALL

INGREDIENTS

200g chocolate, about 35–50% cocoa solids

100g butter

60ml golden syrup

175g peanuts, roughly chopped

50g Rice Krispies

100g Maltesers, roughly chopped

50g Marietta biscuits, roughly broken into pieces

If making into a cake: 50g milk chocolate, melted

METHOD

If making into squares, line a Swiss-roll tin with greaseproof paper. If making for a cake, line a small pudding bowl with a double layer of cling film.

In a heavy-based saucepan, melt the chocolate, butter, and golden syrup over a low heat. Stir regularly to ensure that everything is melting evenly. Take off the heat once fully melted.

Put the peanuts, Rice Krispies, Maltesers and biscuits into a large bowl.

Pour over the melted chocolate mixture and stir well to combine.

Transfer straight into the baking tin or pudding bowl, and smooth over the top.

Refrigerate for at least 2 hours or overnight to set.

When set, for the squares, cut into fingers. For the cake, remove from the bowl, place on a serving plate and drizzle over the melted chocolate and decorate with a 'boom!' sign.

Serves 20

Home
NURSE

Ireland is an ageing nation, and in many households there is an older member of the family being cared for. Caring for an invalid or someone convalescing often requires the planning of separate meals, as their nutritional needs will be altered due to their medical circumstances. When one is unwell, be it a common ailment, a serious condition, recovering from an operation or generally weak of body, it is essential that nutritionally rich foods are taken regularly. Quite often, however, it is at the times when the body needs nutrition the most that it will reject any notion of food. Small portions of nutrient-rich meals are important for the convalescent. Eggs in most forms are a perfect option: a poached, boiled or scrambled egg on wholemeal toast would make for an appetisingly nutritious breakfast, lunch or tea. It is always important to avoid highly spiced, sweetened or greasy foods. At times when all food is unappealing, encourage lots of fluids and slowly try to reintroduce nutrition in the form of freshly juiced fruit or easily digested soup. It is vital that all of these meals are made from perfectly fresh ingredients.

Having four children and an extended family nearby, we rarely get by a couple of months without someone being unwell. The most common household illnesses in a home with small children are the seasonal colds and the dreaded vomiting bug. I have listed some treatments in this chapter, but it is important, especially with a bug, to in some way isolate it and prevent it from spreading to the whole family. My own father can have bouts of illness, and even though his diet is normally relatively good, it can vary according to what is happening with him medically. I found my job as a nurse very fulfilling, but taking care of those you love is heart-warmingly good for the soul. To know that you've made someone's day a little better, or easier in some way, can often give you the best feeling in the world.

Throughout my life there has been a very important family member who has needed care, and I'm certain that his presence in my life has made me a better person.

Nicholas is a young man who has been a part of my family since I was ten years of age. What started out as a little toddler coming for visits along with my sister Fiona, who was working as a care assistant in Nick's care home, turned into a love affair with the whole family. He stole our hearts, and none more than my mother's. His big, brown eyes and everlasting smile had us all smitten. His happiness knew no bounds, and to this day he is still full of laughter and such a joy to be around. Within a short space of time my parents went down the route of fostering, and Nick became an integral part of the family. Nick has cerebral palsy and since he was four years of age he has lived with the Camphill Community in Kilkenny. They are a fantastic organisation that does amazing work with the physically and mentally disabled. Nick would come to stay with us for his holidays, and when my mother became ill, he began holidaying between my sister Fiona's house and mine. My children always welcome Nick with open arms and overload him with kindness, and chocolate, while he is on his stay.

Nick is unable to speak, but we communicate perfectly. His mischievous ways and good humour are so uplifting. He's always happy, and the simplest of things can bring him joy. Each time he is being lifted into the car he can hardly catch his breath with the pure anticipation of where the car journey may take him. He giggles along with the boys when they start discussing some form of toilet humour at the kitchen table. He has a magic sparkle in his eyes when he catches a glimpse of some chocolate cake, knowing it'll be making its way to his plate. This young man has the ability to light up the room without saying a word, and I absolutely love him and his wonderful positivity. When he gives me a big hug before going to sleep at night, he will always make eye contact and I know somehow he's saying 'I love you too'. He's a constant reminder to me that life can be great, no matter what, and I'm truly honoured to have this beautiful person as a part of our family.

Taking care of a loved one, whether they are only sick for the day or if they have a more serious illness, can be extremely fulfilling. At some stage in our lives there will be someone who needs our care, and I feel this is not so much a chore or an obligation but a privilege. The feeling of self-worth and just to know that you are doing something good for somebody can make you feel mighty fine. Most of all, I feel ever grateful to actually have the abilities to make a difference for somebody else.

NATURAL REMEDIES FOR COMMON AILMENTS

I'm a trained nurse, and I have worked in many different areas of nursing and have come into contact with varied illnesses and conditions. Naturally my nursing background has made me a more confident 'home nurse', although a medical background can often go out the window when faced with a medical emergency, especially when the one unwell is a loved one. In every home a little knowledge on the home treatments of common illnesses is essential. For non-serious conditions I generally revert not to my medical background but to remedies and methods that my mother would have used when I was a child. To this day they still prove effective in the treatment of everyday ailments.

BURN / SCALD

A burn is actually different from a scald, but home treatment for each is the same. A burn is caused by dry heat, such as a hot saucepan, whereas a scald is caused by moist heat, such as boiling water or oil. Submerge the burn / scald in a basin of cold water, or place under running cold water. Once the burning subsides, dry with a clean towel. An effective treatment for a burn / scald is aloe vera, so place a little on the affected area, top with a paraffin gauze square and bandage lightly using a dry dressing. Aloe vera is available to buy in pharmacies, but the sap taken from a broken aloe vera leaf is most effective. If it is a bad burn or scald seek medical help.

BEE STING

A bee sting is acidic so must be treated with an alkaline solution. A paste made from bread soda and water is most effective.

WASP STING

A wasp sting is alkaline so must be treated with an acidic solution. Either vinegar or lemon juice is most effective.

NETTLE STING

Rubbing a dock leaf over the affected area will always relieve a nettle sting.

HEAD LICE

Dabbing a little Tea tree oil behind the ears each morning, before school, should keep the head lice away.

EARACHE

Lying on the unaffected side, apply a few drops of warm, but not hot, olive oil to the affected ear, using a dropper or teaspoon, then plug the ear with cotton wool. If the pain doesn't ease, or if there is a discharge from the ear, seek medical attention.

GASTROENTERITIS

To minimise the effects of vomiting, avoid eating for 24hrs, but if at all possible sip on cooled boiled water to avoid dehydration. Avoid carbonated drinks, even if flat, as the sugar has an osmotic effect on the gut and in turn can cause an even more severe dehydration. If vomiting persists, or is accompanied by a high temperature, seek medical help.

To minimise the effects of diarrhoea, it is vital to drink plenty of fluids, but as the body is losing essential electrolytes these need to be replaced. Supplements are available in the pharmacy, but if tolerated, potassium-packed bananas are helpful to the gut. It's important that all milk and dairy products be avoided until back to normal, as they will aggravate the bowel. If diarrhoea is severe or lasts more than a couple of days contact a doctor.

BAD BREATH {HALITOSIS}

Chewing on a small handful of fresh parsley can help to freshen the breath due to the chemical presence of chlorophyll in the parsley.

CHICKEN POX

Oatmeal baths can sooth the itching caused by chicken pox. Place a handful of oats into a gauze bag, or make a bag using a square of muslin, and while running the bath water let it hang under the running tap.

BRUISES

Some cotton wool soaked with witch hazel and then applied to the bruise should ease its severity.

HOUSEHOLD VIRUSES

When there is a contagious illness, such as gastroenteritis, in a home, an onion cut in half and left on the countertop has the ability to absorb some of the germs lurking in the house, which can reduce the risk of others contracting the illness.

HOARSENESS

Take a spoonful of honey straight from the spoon.

SORE THROAT

Relieve a sore throat with Thyme and Sage Tea. Allow 2 sprigs of thyme and 5 sage leaves to infuse in 275 ml of boiling water. Strain, allow to cool and then gargle.

FIRST AID BOX

A well-stocked first aid box is imperative for any kitchen. For simple first aid procedures that don't require medical assistance, it is important to have a well-stocked first aid box that is easily accessible, but always ensure that it is either locked or completely out of children's reach.

- Antiseptic lotion – such as Dettol
- Sterile cotton wool
- Sterile dressing
- A crepe bandage
- Assorted plasters
- Small scissors
- Paraffin gauze squares, for dressing burns / scalds or grazes
- Tweezers
- Thermometer. A digital one is perfect; just ensure that it always has working batteries
- Antihistamine tablets and syrup
- Aloe vera lotion. Otherwise an Aloe vera plant on the window sill
- Arnica ointment, which is very effective in easing the severity of a bruise
- Peppermint tablets – they work best for indigestion
- Calamine lotion
- Medicine to treat common family illnesses, such as paracetamol for a temperature

HOME-MADE COLD REMEDY

As a child, once there was a chance of a sniffle in the house, my mother would always rely on a home-made citrus drink of freshly squeezed lemons and oranges to warn away further symptoms of the cold. It always seemed to give some relief, and to this day I still make this drink when the signs of a cold are upon us. My remedy is based on my mother's drink, and even though it won't get rid of the cold it will certainly help to mitigate some of the symptoms.

Winter is the season when it's to be expected that every second person has some symptoms or other of a cold. We naturally blame the weather, which does play its part in aiding sickness, however it is not the cold weather of winter that causes the common cold but rather the fact that through the winter months we tend to spend a lot more time indoors in close proximity to each other. This then accommodates the spreading of the cold virus very conveniently. So it's no surprise that many children in crèches and school are most prone to acquiring the symptoms of a cold. This thought always makes me feel justified when swinging open the windows on a freezing cold day to let some crisp fresh air into the house.

The symptoms of the common cold most often don't warrant any doctor's intervention. It's a viral condition that won't benefit from any antibiotic treatment, but that miserable feeling of a stuffy head, sore throat, blocked nose, an irritating cough and profuse sneezing will often require some home remedies to ease these complaints, while helping to aid a speedier recovery. The ingredients of this drink have all merited their place in this virus-fighting concoction. Lemons are among a group of foods that are best for boosting the immune system and balancing the body's acid and alkali pH. Like oranges they are high in Vitamin C, which is a powerful antioxidant that helps to fight off infections and helps the body to repair cells at times of sickness. At the onset of a cold, increasing one's intake of Vitamin C can ease its severity or even stop its onset. It has also been well documented that honey and ginger both help the immune system and are recommended for times when one is feeling a little run down. I have plenty of mint growing in the garden, which mostly survives the cold weather, so I tend to use it a lot for herbal teas. A few sprigs make a wonderful addition to this drink, as mint has the ability to sooth the digestive tract and subsequently ease any tummy aches. When one is under the weather it is always important to keep hydrated, so this drink, along with all of its nutrient-rich ingredients, makes for the perfect tonic!

INGREDIENTS

Juice of 1 orange

Juice of half a lemon

1 tbsp honey

1 inch knob of ginger,
  peeled and chopped

4 mint leaves (optional)

METHOD

Juice the orange and
lemon into a pint glass.

Add the honey, ginger and
mint. Top up with boiling
water and stir well.

Allow to sit for 10 minutes,
then pass through a sieve
for a smooth drink.

Taste, and add more
honey if required.

CARRAGEEN
MOSS PUDDING

Carrageen Moss, which is also known as Irish moss, is a type of seaweed that has been used for hundreds of years as a natural thickening agent in cooking. Like most seaweeds, Carrageen is highly nutritious as it is packed with vitamins, minerals and nutrients. It is very rich in iron, iodine and fibre and is a powerful antioxidant. Always complimented for its high nutritional content, Carrageen moss is recommended in many old recipe books from the last century as an important supplementary food for the sick. It was mostly endorsed as a tonic, with a handful of the Carrageen popped into a mug of hot water with a spoonful of sugar, and taken as a highly nutritious drink. To make it more appetising, however, using it in a creamy pudding was generally the favoured serving suggestion. In recent times Carrageen has been making a comeback, not only as a dietary supplement but also on the menu of some very prestigious restaurants.

We are fortunate in Ireland to have an abundance of wonderful health-benefiting seaweed, free for the taking, from any of our beautiful shores. The best time to forage for Carrageen moss is during mid to late spring. It is important to cut the seaweed with a knife and only take one leaf from each plant, leaving the stalk and blade, which will allow for regrowth of the plant. Rinse the seaweed under running water then leave to dry completely outside in the sun in a single layer on some sort of rack. Don't worry if you don't get the opportunity to find your own Carrageen moss, as it can be found fairly commonly in most health food shops and also online. Whether foraged or bought, when in its dried form the Carrageen moss will keep almost indefinitely.

This Carrageen moss pudding is quite similar to set custard, but is much lighter due to the lesser quantity of egg yolks included, and each spoonful is perfectly fluffy while almost melting on the tongue. The creamy nature of the pudding is best served with a little tart stewed fruit, such as rhubarb.

INGREDIENTS

7g cleaned, well-dried
Carrageen Moss

700ml milk

200ml cream

1tsp of vanilla extract

2tbsp of castor sugar

1 egg

METHOD

Soak the carrageen in a small bowl
of tepid water for 10 minutes.

Strain off the water and put the
carrageen into a saucepan with
milk, cream and vanilla extract.

Bring to the boil and then simmer very
gently on a low heat for 20 minutes.

When the milk is ready, separate
the egg into two bowls, put the yolk
into a large bowl, add the sugar and
whisk together for a few seconds.

Pour the creamy milk and carrageen moss
through a sieve, with a spoon pressing
against the sieve to extract all the jelly-like
substance from the carrageen, onto the
egg yolk mixture whisking continuously.

In a separate bowl, whisk the egg
white until stiff and fold it in gently
to the carrageen mixture.

Either pour into individual cups or one
big serving bowl. The pudding was
traditionally eaten straight away while
still warm, but is nicer when left to cool
and set in the fridge for 2–3 hours.

Serve chilled with softly whipped
cream and some stewed fruit.

Serves 6

SUMMER VITAMIN BOOST

In summer it can often seem easier to have a good intake of vitamins and minerals as there is generally an abundance of deliciously ripe and beautifully coloured fruit and vegetables in our gardens, markets and shops. Our kitchen island is home to a large fruit basket, which tends to complement the season with whatever fruit I can get my hands on. When thoughts turn to the possibility of a snack, however, quite often this beautiful display can simply be mistaken for a pretty kitchen prop and bypassed, and admittedly it's not only the children who are guilty of this. I do find it very useful to have some fruit washed and ready to chop at a moment's notice of a rumbling belly. There is something about a bowl of freshly chopped fruit served with little forks and accompanying bowls of creamy Greek yogurt that children really enjoy.

When I've a little time on my hands, and the fruit in the basket is plentiful and ripe, I love to make some use out of my juicer, and make this highly nutritious juice drink. The combination that I use normally depends upon what fruit I have at hand or what vegetables are in the garden, but this juice drink is our current favourite.

Carrots are one vegetable that juices very easily, and adds a delicious sweetness to any juice drink. Carrots have an especially high level of Vitamin A. This vitamin is essential for good eyesight, specifically in dim light. During World War II the British championed this belief by declaring that British pilots improved their night vision by eating vast amounts of carrots. They were, however, only trying to encourage the eating of carrots, as it was one of the few foods that were not in short supply during the war, and the fact that it may have aided their vision was a bonus.

Vitamin A is found fortified in many food products such as cereals and breads, but to eat the raw version, as in carrots, is much more beneficial to one's health. Quite shockingly, a recent report from the World Health Organisation states that almost 1.4 million children worldwide are blind solely due to the lack of access to any form of Vitamin A.

This drink would also serve well as an immunity booster, and would be especially beneficial if summer colds were lurking.

INGREDIENTS

8 large carrots,
washed and peeled

4 apples, quartered
and cored

2 oranges, peeled
and segmented

¼ of a pineapple,
peeled, cored and
cut into pieces

METHOD

Using an electric juice extractor,
press each ingredient through,
collecting the juice.

Alternatively, if you do not have a juicer,
liquidise the hard fruit, juice the citrus
fruits and then pass the contents through
a sieve collecting all the juicy goodness.

To best benefit from all the
vitamins and minerals within the
drink, enjoy straight away.

Serves 2

Steaming fish will often result in the fish being cooked more delicately, which in turn makes it a little easier to digest. This makes it an ideal dish for someone with a delicate tummy or for times when one is convalescing. A parsley sauce makes a wonderful accompaniment to any sort of fish and adds great flavour to this dish, which is so simply cooked. When buying fish ensure that it is perfectly fresh, which means no fishy smell whatsoever.

STEAMED FISH WITH A PARSLEY SAUCE

INGREDIENTS

50g butter

1 onion, finely diced

50g plain flour

400ml warm milk

Salt and pepper

2tbsp finely chopped flat leaf parsley

4 fillets of whiting

1 lemon, cut into wedges

METHOD

Firstly make the parsley sauce. Melt the butter in a medium-sized saucepan, add the diced onion and sweat for about 10 minutes, until the onions are soft but not coloured.

Using a wooden spoon, add the flour and stir for 2 minutes to allow the flour to cook a little.

Turn up the heat and slowly add the warmed milk. Stirring constantly, bring to the boil then simmer for a minute. Season with a little salt and pepper and stir in the chopped parsley. Take off the heat but cover to keep warm.

Place the fish pieces, skin side down, into the bottom portion of the steamer. Cook for 10–12 minutes, depending on the size of the fillet, until the fish is cooked through and flaky.

Serve immediately, with a good drizzle of parsley sauce over each fillet of fish, and a sprinkling of chopped parsley and a wedge of lemon on the side.

Serves 4

GINGERBREAD

The bond between mother and child is something so strong that time can never lessen. My father has so many stories about the wonderful lady his mother was, the fun times she shared with her children, the cakes she would bake, the gardens she took care of, but most of all how she delivered such kindness. His memories are so strong that even as a man of 81 he talks of his mother as though he had only spent the day with her yesterday. Sadly it has been over seventy years since his mother passed away, but her positive influence, in his early years, shaped him into the man he became and still is. I would always describe my father as an individual with a strong character, but ever so kind in nature. With obvious similarities from mother to son, it hasn't been difficult for me to picture this beautiful kind lady of whom he speaks so fondly.

My father was the youngest of five, and has many memories of helping his mother in the kitchen. He recalls the baking of the weekly cake – something that would require the skills of a young keen helper, as vigorous stirring of the cake mixture was necessary. On alternate weeks either a caraway cake or gingerbread would be baked. The anticipation for the gingerbread was always greater than the caraway. This cake would then last almost the week long, with it being evenly rationed between all in the house. Similar to my story with the search for the scone recipe, my father has often dreamed of uncovering this gingerbread recipe; however it has always been in vain. A few years ago we discovered a box of old handwritten recipes. Amongst these was a domestic science copybook, dated 1902, belonging to Mary Kate O'Connell, Dad's mother. This may or may not have been the recipe that she had used in her family kitchen, but it was worth a try. I baked it according to the instructions, but just multiplied the ingredients by two, poured it in a 2lb loaf tin and my father earnestly awaited a sample. I eagerly awaited his verdict. His eyes filled with tears and he told me that it did taste similar to the childhood cake he remembered. On seeing his sorrow, I realised that the most important ingredient needed for that nostalgic gingerbread, and the strongest element to this lasting cake memory, was missing: his mother.

Ginger Bread.

<u>Ingredients.</u>

6 ozs flour
$\frac{1}{4}$ lb treacle } 1

1 oz butter
1 " sugar
1 Egg } 2

$\frac{1}{2}$ tea. sp. ground ginger
$\frac{1}{4}$ " " soda.
2 table. sp milk
$\frac{1}{2}$ oz candied peel. } $\frac{3}{4}$

$3\frac{3}{4}$

<u>Method.</u>   Add ginger and peel to the flour. Melt the sugar, butter and treacle in a saucepan Mix the soda milk and egg. Make a well in the centre of the flour pour in the treacle etc, and the egg, milk and soda. Stir quickly and put in some greased patty pans half full. Bake in a moderately hot oven 10 to 15 mins.

Richmond Cakes

<u>Ingred.</u>

$\frac{1}{2}$ lb flour   1
pinch of salt
3 ozs lard,   } $1\frac{1}{2}$
4 " sugar
4 " currants   } 1

2 Eggs
$\frac{1}{2}$ tea cup of milk } 3
$\frac{1}{2}$ tea sp. of B. Powder

$6\frac{1}{2}$

There is something so comforting about the ambrosial vanilla scent of custard. The home-made variety is actually quite easy to make, tastes divine and considering it's mostly milk and eggs, is rather nutritious. Custard is especially suited to someone convalescing due to its palatable taste, ease to swallow and good calorie content. To add to its flavour and texture some tart, stewed fruit pairs very nicely with the creamy sweet vanilla custard.

VANILLA CUSTARD & STEWED APPLE

INGREDIENTS

Stewed Apple

500g Bramley apples

50g caster sugar

1 tbsp water

Custard:

500ml milk {or a mixture of milk & cream}

1 tsp vanilla extract

4 egg yolks

50g caster sugar

METHOD

To stew the apples, core, peel and slice the apples and place into a medium saucepan with the sugar and water. When it comes to the boil, reduce the heat and simmer for 5 minutes, until the apple has broken down but there are still a few chunks remaining. Remove from the heat, taste and add more sugar if necessary.

Place a saucepan over a low heat, and pour in the milk and vanilla extract. Gently heat to a low simmer, stirring constantly.

In a bowl, whisk the egg yolks with the sugar until pale and creamy.

Slowly pour the hot milk into the egg mixture, whisking as you pour.

Then pour back into a clean saucepan. Place over a low heat and cook for 3–4 minutes, constantly stirring with a wooden spoon until the custard begins to thicken. If left beyond this point the custard will become lumpy. Remove immediately from the heat and pour into a serving jug.

Serves 4

A good mug of herbal tea can be easily achieved once you have a few herbs from the garden, and these home-brewed varieties are a lot more refreshing than the ready-made herbal teabags. Fresh herbs are bursting with vitamins, minerals and antioxidants, so when combined with boiling water they provide a very nutritious alternative to your normal cup of tea or coffee. My favourite herbal tea would have to be a simple mint tea, but there are some other combinations that I enjoy and each offer wonderful health benefits. As with anything, drink these teas in moderation, and seek the advice of a doctor before doing so if pregnant or on medication.

HERB GARDEN TEAS

Peppermint/Spearmint Tea – 10 leaves
Sooths stomach problems and aids digestion.

Lemon balm Tea – 10 leaves
Helps to calm & eases sleep.

Thyme Tea – 2 sprigs plus juice of half a
lemon and a squeeze of honey makes a powerful cold remedy. Thyme is recommended for its anti-inflammatory properties.

Rosemary Tea – 2 sprigs
Can help to ease allergies such as hay fever. It is also good for concentration as it is said to increase the blood flow to the brain.

Tarragon Tea – 2 sprigs
Can ease the effect of a chesty cough.

Basil Tea – 10 leaves, freshly chopped
Anti-inflammatory properties.

Sage Tea – 2 sprigs
Helps with bloating at time of a monthly cycle.

Lavender Tea – 2 sprigs
Can be sipped as a relaxing brew, or allow to cool and use to sooth insect bites and minor burns of the skin.

Dandelion Tea – 2 yellow dandelion heads
Dandelions are not a herb, but if like me you have children who can't pass a dandelion clock without blowing it, you're sure to have plenty around the place. Dandelions are a known diuretic and are a powerful antioxidant.

METHOD

Using a bowl, flask or teapot, add the herbs of your choice and cover with 275ml of boiling water.

Leave to infuse for 10 mins. Then strain using a little sieve and enjoy straight away.

Serves 1

LAVENDER-INFUSED HONEY

A little honey is always most welcome in a cup of herbal tea. For a fragrant touch to a jar of ordinary honey, simply add a few sprigs of fresh lavender. Leave to infuse for at least 1 week before enjoying.

IMMUNE-BOOSTING JUICE

Early spring 2011 was a very bleak time for our family. My aunt Judy, whom we greatly loved, passed away after a relatively short battle with cancer. Within a few days we were to be given news so awful that I'm sure to never forget the shock I felt on hearing it. My sister Dervilla was diagnosed with breast cancer. In all my time of friends and relatives becoming sick, this news hit me the hardest. It was completely inconceivable that a young woman with three small children, my sister, could be diagnosed with this unpredictable disease. As a mother the pressure was always on her to keep the good side out. She did everything possible to maintain life as normal as she could, for her children's sake. It was something that may not have come easily to her, but she excelled at it. For the year of her treatments I found her daily positivity enlightening. She wanted to stay strong and she was truly confident that through each step of her treatment she was that bit closer to full recovery. She was fighting back at the cancer with every good cell in her body.

When cancer hits a family it is soul shattering, since as an illness it is so precarious. When someone close to you is seriously unwell, the feeling of helplessness is devastating. You want to make things right. You want to completely reassure and say that of course they are going to be one of the lucky ones, but in your heart you don't really know, and this is unbelievably heartbreaking. However it was Dervilla's own positivity, her unbelievable positivity, which made me truly believe that she was going to get through this, and she did. In recent years there have been many advances made with the treatment of cancers, and thankfully so many more are now standing up to cancer and surviving it.

For the weeks while Dervilla was on chemotherapy there was little food she could tolerate. Most food was unpalatable, but getting some strength from it was essential. She was advised to buy a juicing machine, and in a bid to maintain any sort of energy she would juice and drink lots of different fruit combinations daily. They were made in minutes, easy to swallow and thankfully gave fairly sufficient nutrients. She actually still makes these juices, and I'm sure there is immense comfort that these nutritionally rich drinks are now being taken by choice and not by compulsion. I'm overjoyed that Dervilla is back to a happy and healthy state, and that life for her is good again.

INGREDIENTS

3 carrots

1 stick of celery

1 apple

½ a handful wheatgrass

METHOD

Using an electric juice extractor, press each ingredient through, individually, collecting the juice.

Serves 1

FOOD

for the

GREAT

OUTDOORS

The highlight of my childhood summers was the fortnightly visit to Galway, where a day at the beach would be spent. A large hamper, tightly packed with assorted sandwiches, tea, and if we had been especially good, biscuit cake, would be part of our car boot picnic. Then hours were spent splashing in the water and walking the long length of the beach collecting shells and pebbles. The journey home would always include the obligatory bag of chipper chips. The anticipation for carefully opening that vinegar-soaked brown parcel was almost as great as dipping the first toe into the sea earlier that day. Once the chips were consumed and we were homeward bound, tiredness would set in.

These were the days before sun cream and when travelling home from the beach would involve a balancing act on the seat, for fear of brushing your third-degree burns off anything. Those childhood summer days, even though spent quite simply, and even with the stinging of sunburn still in mind, bring back endless happy memories to me. Some might say it was a sign of the times and that life was less complicated back then, but I'd have to disagree. My own children would now relish such a day, minus the sunburn naturally. The happiest of times and the most beautiful memories are created not in extravagant ways but by the people we choose to spend these times with.

A family picnic is one outing that I enjoy the most with my own children. An exotic location isn't paramount. Even the idea of setting up a picnic in the back garden is met with lots of excitement. Once there is the promise of a clear sky and a little heat in the air, a picnic makes for a fabulous way to spend some time together.

PACKING THE PERFECT PICNIC

There are many perfect locations for setting up a picnic: on the beach, in a park, in the back garden, or my favourite would have to be in a freshly cut meadow.

A must for all picnics is a large blanket to sit on, cushions also if you are planning on really indulging in an afternoon of relaxation al fresco. Plastic plates, cups and cutlery, kitchen paper, some wet wipes and a plastic bag for rubbish are all an essential part of the picnic hamper. I adore wicker picnic baskets and would happily transport my groceries in one, just for the sheer look of it, however cool bags or boxes can be a more practical approach. If taking a track and walking a distance to the desired picnic area, it can be advantageous to leave the basket or box at home and in its place use a backpack for transporting the picnic. Whichever is the chosen method for carrying the food, it is best to line the base with freezer blocks. All precooked foods should be refrigerated until ready to leave the house. When packing the picnic food the raw ingredients are best placed at the bottom and naturally the more fragile ones nearer the top. To keep the food fresh I tend to wrap sandwiches, rolls and pies in greaseproof paper then in tin foil. Cakes and biscuits I normally transport in a tin, all drinks or dressings in plastic bottles or flasks, and any food that has the possibility of leaking I ensure is transported in a tightly sealed container.

A PICNIC WITH A DIFFERENCE

If time is on your side, and a feeling of creativity is upon you, a very wonderful addition to a picnic is a campfire. The setting up of a campfire is something that brings great excitement to a picnic, and for some it can be a fabulous way to embrace the hunter–gatherer inside. I would never have contemplated such a task, and in fact would have found it more than daunting when I had a babe in arms, yet once the children are of a reasonable age this has been something that both they and I have enjoyed.

A wire grate isn't essential, yet I find it to be rather convenient for placing over the coals, once they are hot enough to cook on. A ring of stones must first be put in place for the campfire, which should not be wider than the grill you intend to use. This will contain the fire while also acting as a balance for the grill. The experienced campers will profess that dry twigs, leaves and a few matches are sufficient for starting a fire, yet I like the reassurance of knowing that I have a few firelighters to the ready if all else fails.

The food need not be complicated to create a campfire feast. I have included some of my favourite campfire recipes, but even a packet of sausages, a little oil and an old frying pan would suffice as a very adventurous addition to the picnic menu. In the past, according to my children, these sausages have tasted better than any I have ever made before. However I somehow get the feeling if I were to plate up charred sausages at the kitchen table they may be sent straight back to me.

It's important to always have safety in mind when building a campfire. Never build near flammable materials, and ensure that the campfire is situated a good distance from tents, dry leaves, overhanging branches, trees and their roots. The handles of saucepans will get very hot, so ensure that you have an oven glove packed. Also be especially careful when children are playing nearby. As an extra safety measure, have a bucket of water on standby, and when finished with the campfire take care that it is completely extinguished before leaving the campsite.

Dining outdoors, be it a barbecue, campfire or picnic, can be as simple or as elaborate as you please. We have often taken off with a picnic bag containing nothing more than some bread, fruit and something to drink. When lots of excitement and imagination are in tow, the possibility of a great day out is always guaranteed.

In the past few years, since having our own hens in the garden, I have become a serious egg fan. The flavour, colour and texture to farm eggs, as known by many, is incomparable to the shop-bought variety. A simple boiled egg makes for a wonderful nutritious start to the day. Whipping a few eggs together to make a quiche adds a little indulgence to the already tasty eggs. There is no need to season the egg mixture with salt, as the addition of the bacon provides enough salt for the dish. I have yet to decide if I prefer this quiche served hot or cold. When hot, the melted cheese and crispy bacon ooze from the case, and when cold the eggs and cheese have completely set and all the flavours seem to develop a little more. If having a lunch, or picnic, based around salads, a quiche makes for a perfectly flavoursome alternative to cold meats.

SPINACH & BACON QUICHE

INGREDIENTS

Shortcrust pastry

200g plain flour, sifted

Pinch of salt

100g chilled
butter, cubed

1 egg yolk (beaten)

1 tbsp cold water

Filling

2 eggs and 2 egg yokes

150ml milk

150ml cream

1 tbsp chopped chives

100g Cheddar
cheese, grated

Freshly ground
black pepper

60g baby spinach leaves

175g streaky bacon,
cooked and roughly
chopped

METHOD

Preheat the oven to 200°C / fan 180°C / Gas Mark 6. Grease a 23cm (9in) shallow flan tin.

Place the flour, salt and butter in a food processor and whiz briefly. Add half the beaten egg and continue to whiz. You might add a little more egg, but not too much as the mixture should be just moist enough to come together.

If making by hand, sieve the flour and pinch of salt into a bowl. Rub the butter into the flour until it resembles breadcrumbs. Add the egg yolk and bring it together to form dough. If the mixture is too dry, add a tbsp. of cold water.

Flatten out the dough ball and wrap it in cling film, then leave it in the fridge for 30 minutes or, if in a hurry, in the freezer for 10 minutes.

On a floured surface, roll out the pastry to fit the prepared tin. Then carefully line the tin with the pastry. Cover the base with parchment paper and fill the tin with baking beans then bake 'blind' for 10 minutes.

Remove the paper and beans and return to the oven for a further 2 minutes, before setting to one side until the filling is ready.

For the filling, whisk the eggs in a medium-sized bowl; add the milk and cream, chives and cheese. Mix well and add seasoning.

Layer the spinach and rashers into the pastry base. Pour the egg mixture over and return to the oven for 30 minutes, or until the centre has set. Serve warm or cold with a green salad and some home-made soda bread.

Serves 6–8

These little wraps make the perfect picnic food, as they travel very well in a cooled picnic basket. The chicken is lightly spiced yet mild enough for young children to enjoy, due to the addition of the cooling yogurt. This, along with a crisp salad, is a delicious filling for soft tortilla wraps. They can be served simply cut in half, but I find the pinwheels are especially appealing to the younger family members, especially if bringing on a picnic or for the school lunchbox. They are easy for little hands to manage and take less time to eat than a sandwich, which means more time for playing.

CHICKEN TIKKA PINWHEELS

INGREDIENTS

150g Greek yogurt

Juice of 1 lime

2 cloves of garlic, crushed

1 tsp garam masala

¼ tsp turmeric

¼ tsp chilli powder

Freshly ground pepper

4 chicken fillets, butterflied

To Serve:

6 flour tortilla wraps

3 tbsp mayonnaise

1 little gem lettuce

2 tomatoes

METHOD

To a large bowl, add the Greek yogurt, lime juice, garlic, garam masala, turmeric, chilli powder and a few grinds of black pepper.

Add the chicken fillets and coat each one well with the marinade. Leave to marinade in the fridge for 2 hours or if possible overnight.

Arrange the chicken on a foil-lined grill rack and cook for about 5 minutes on each side, until cooked through and slightly golden.

Warm the tortilla wraps in the microwave. Cover one side of each wrap with a little mayonnaise. Slice up the chicken and divide among the tortilla wraps. Scatter over some lettuce and slices of tomato.

Roll the wraps up tightly, then slice diagonally into bite-size pieces. Wrap in greaseproof paper ready for the picnic box.

Serves 6

Often when bringing along some chopped fruit on a picnic they can become a little overheated and in turn become somewhat mushy. Of course ice packs neatly nestled around the fruit containers can be beneficial for keeping everything at a nice temperature, but will they look as impressive as a frozen melon bowl? I think not!

For a rather impressive and very convenient fruit salad transporter, a frozen, scooped-out melon works a treat. It will keep the fruit chilled for hours. Just remember to pack some cocktail sticks or forks so everyone can enjoy some chilled fruit from this communal fruit bowl.

MELON ICE BOWL WITH FRUIT SALAD

INGREDIENTS

1 honeydew melon

150g strawberries, cut in half

150g blueberries

150g grapes, cut in half

1 tbsp caster sugar

1 tbsp chopped fresh mint

METHOD

Cut the melon in half horizontally. Spoon out the seeds, then carefully, using a sharp knife, remove the flesh and reserve it in a bowl.

Place the honeydew melon shells in the freezer for 3–4 hours or overnight.

Chop the reserved melon flesh. Place in a bowl with the strawberries, blueberries and grapes. Sprinkle over the sugar and stir in the mint.

Mix together and spoon into the frozen melon shells. To transport cover tightly with cling film then tin foil and sit upright in the picnic basket.

Serves 6

I grew up with a serious love of chocolate biscuit cake. For as long as I can remember, the most popular treat that my mother would make was her famous chocolate biscuit cake. Never was there a birthday party or a family gathering but a large tray of it was on offer. It was a perfectly simple recipe, and a lot less luscious than my own version, however it is still a recipe I use to this day. Jack loves orange-flavoured chocolate, and he also loved my Mam's biscuit cake. So for his eighth birthday I developed this recipe. The invigorating zestiness of orange along with the creamy chocolate gives such a wonderful depth of flavour to this cake. It is incredibly indulgent, so a little finger per serving will suffice. It benefits greatly from resting, tightly parcelled, in the fridge, so only pack in the picnic hamper just before leaving the house.

CHOCOLATE ORANGE BISCUIT CAKE

INGREDIENTS

300g Marietta biscuits

250g good quality dark chocolate (60% cocoa solids)

100g butter, melted

1tsp drinking chocolate

½tsp of orange extract

1 tin condensed milk

Topping:

100g milk chocolate, melted

½ an orange, zest only

METHOD

Roughly crush the biscuits in a bowl.

Melt the chocolate, butter and drinking chocolate together in a large bowl over a saucepan of simmering water. Remove from the heat, and then stir in the orange extract and condensed milk.

Pour this chocolate mixture over the bowl of biscuits and stir well to combine all the ingredients.

Line a 2lb loaf tin with cling film (or baking parchment) and spoon the mixture into it. Place the tin in the fridge to set for at least 2 hours.

Place on a serving plate and drizzle with the melted chocolate and grate over the zest of half an orange. The cake will keep in the fridge for 3 days.

When one of my young men was very little he went through a huge Barney phase. No matter what we were doing in our daily lives there seemed to be an appropriate Barney jingle. Barney seemed to sing a lot about these s'mores, but I had never even heard of them let alone tasted them. However, I must say he sold the idea of them pretty well to me. So one wintry evening, using the open fire in place of the campfire, we made Barney's s'mores and had our own sitting room campfire.

These chocolate and marshmallow toasties are based on the s'mores concept. They can be assembled before the picnic or camping trip. Wrapped in some bbq tinfoil or two layers of the ordinary tin foil, they'll be ready for whenever needed. I'm not quite sure these days if any of my young men would join me in a chorus of Barney's campfire tunes, but none of them would refuse one of these chocolatey, gooey creations. If not out adventuring but in the comfort of your own kitchen, these toasties can be popped on a griddle pan, and for an extra touch of indulgence top with a spoonful of vanilla ice-cream.

CHOCOLATE & MARSHMALLOW S'MORE TOASTIE

INGREDIENTS

2 slices of brioche

Butter for spreading

2 marshmallows, cut in four or 5 mini ones

2 squares of chocolate, grated or thinly sliced

METHOD

Spread some butter on one side of the bread.

Sprinkle some marshmallows and chocolate on one of the unbuttered sides of bread.

Sandwich together with butter side facing up.

Cut a large square of tin foil. Place the sandwich in the centre and tightly fold the foil around it, ensuring there are no gaps for the melted chocolate or marshmallows to escape.

When ready to eat, place the tinfoil package on a grate over the hot coals. Cook on each side for about 2 minutes. Have a little peak in to make sure everything has melted. If not, tighten up the foil again and place it back on the grate for another minute or so.

Carefully unwrap the tin foil package and let it cool a little before tucking in.

Serves 2

As comforting as it is that my older boys are now starting to cook for themselves, somehow they always seem to choose ingredients that I may have bought with a particular use in mind. I love serving naan bread alongside a spicy curry, however more and more recently when I go to the press for that naan I discover it has disappeared. Once questioning ensues, low and behold I find that it was used as a snack the previous evening. If time is short for these men, and by this I mean if a favourite programme is about to begin, they will simply toast it and top with garlic butter. However their favourite use for naan bread is as a base for a pizza, and they will then top it with whatever cheese and cooked meat they can lay their hands upon. Naan bread can also easily be slit open, which reveals a pocket, perfect for stuffing with sauce, cheese and any other already cooked topping of choice. This makes them a rather convenient food to wrap in tin foil and bring along to cook on the campfire, when they happen to taste rather good too.

CAMPFIRE POCKET PIZZA

INGREDIENTS

1 naan bread

2tbsp of any tomato
  based pasta /
  pizza sauce

2tbsp cheese, grated

1 slice of cooked
  ham, chopped

2 fresh chives,
  finely chopped

METHOD

Cut 2 pieces of tin foil, about twice the size of the naan bread.

Open the naan bread by slitting it down the centre.

Spoon in the tomato sauce, evenly covering one side of the naan. Add the cheese, ham, and chives.

Sit the filled naan into the centre of the double layer of tin foil and wrap it up, securing the sides tightly by bunching the tin foil together.

Place on the wire rack of the campfire for 3 minutes on each side. Carefully unwrap and enjoy.

Serves 1

There was complete excitement each year when my father would return from herding cattle only to announce that he had seen the first mushroom of the season. If one was seen, many more were clearly going to be hidden amongst the long clumps of grass. Mushroom-picking season generally began near the summer's end, and continued for what seemed like many weeks into the school year.

We never had anything as impressive as the beautiful baskets today's foragers now possess. Even though in hindsight there was nothing stopping us from bringing a kitchen bowl or even a bag out with us, we always stuck to the more traditional method. A few strong blades of grass on which the mushrooms would be threaded were our method of transporting these foraged fungi from field to kitchen. Most of the mushrooms recovered were the reliable small snow-white variety, but on occasion we would make a glorious find of the larger, flat field mushroom. There was always a great sense of achievement for whoever discovered the stash. The preparation and cooking method for these never much varied. A good sprinkling of salt covered the mushroom before being smeared in butter, with a little extra left in the cap to melt as the mushroom was being cooked. Without the modern day concerns of dirt and germs, they would then be sat straight onto the hot stove until somewhat cooked. These mushrooms were served on top of a chunk of soda bread, which quite nicely would mop up all the buttery juices.

Nowadays, without access to a stove, I generally oven cook my field mushrooms. I do however find that a wonderful way to recreate these treasured caps is by either barbecuing or cooking on a campfire. I'm a real lover of mushrooms as they can hold their own in any dish, due to their robust nature, but the addition of the flavoursome pesto and creamy brie gives enough substance to the mushrooms that it would be served well as a versatile vegetarian burger. This may not be a combination that would have been an option in our 1980s kitchen, yet I still somehow feel nostalgic every time I have these fabulous field mushrooms to hand.

BBQ BRIE & PESTO MUSHROOMS

INGREDIENTS

4 Portobello mushrooms, cleaned and stalks removed

25g butter

Salt and freshly ground pepper

25g butter, soft

2 cloves of garlic, crushed

2tbsp basil pesto

100g brie, cut into 16 chunks

To Serve:

4 slices of brioche

METHOD

Smear a little butter over each mushroom, and season with some salt and pepper. In a bowl, combine the soft butter with the garlic and pesto. Divide the pesto butter between the four mushrooms, then top with the brie. Wrap each mushroom in tin foil, and place in a portable container.

When ready to cook, place the mushrooms in foil on the hot barbeque / campfire rack for about 20 minutes.

When the butter and brie has melted, and the mushroom is cooked through, remove from the barbeque / campfire. Place on a slice of brioche and eat straight away.

Serves 4

When having a barbeque, or indeed have a little campfire lit, it's a real novelty to also cook up some dessert on it. I always have an abundance of berries in the summer months, and as much as I enjoy using them for my home-made jams or eating them on their own, I'm always looking for different ways to use them. Roasted fruit happens to be one of my favourite winter desserts, as any less-than-sweet fruit benefits greatly from roasting alongside a little honey or a sprinkling of sugar. I never limit this dessert to winter, as I have found that to cook them similarly on a barbecue or a campfire produces something so scrumptious you can't resist diving in, even if the sun is splitting the rocks. If bringing along on a picnic, I would leave the assembling of the parcel until at the campfire, to avoid it leaking as you travel. Alternatively to the tin foil parcel, a portable aluminium tin with a lid can be used. If out on an autumn picnic you may happen to stumble upon some wild blackberries that would be wonderful cooked in exactly the same way.

HONEY ROASTED FRUIT PARCEL

INGREDIENTS

500g mixed berries

2 peaches

2 clementines / mandarins

4tsp honey

4tbsp orange juice

To Serve:

Freshly whipped cream

Mint leaves

METHOD

Cut 4 pieces of tin foil, each the size of a dinner plate.

Leave the berries whole, apart from the strawberries, which should be hulled and halved. Slice the peaches. Peel and segment the clementines / mandarins.

Divide the fruit evenly between the four sheets of tin foil. Bunch up the tin foil to make a parcel. Drizzle in a tsp of honey and a tbsp of orange juice into each one.

Tightly seal the parcel, and place on the barbecue / campfire for 6–8 minutes, until the fruit is soft and oozing of juices.

Take from the barbecue / campfire and serve the parcel slightly opened with a dollop of cream and a mint leaf to decorate.

Serves 4

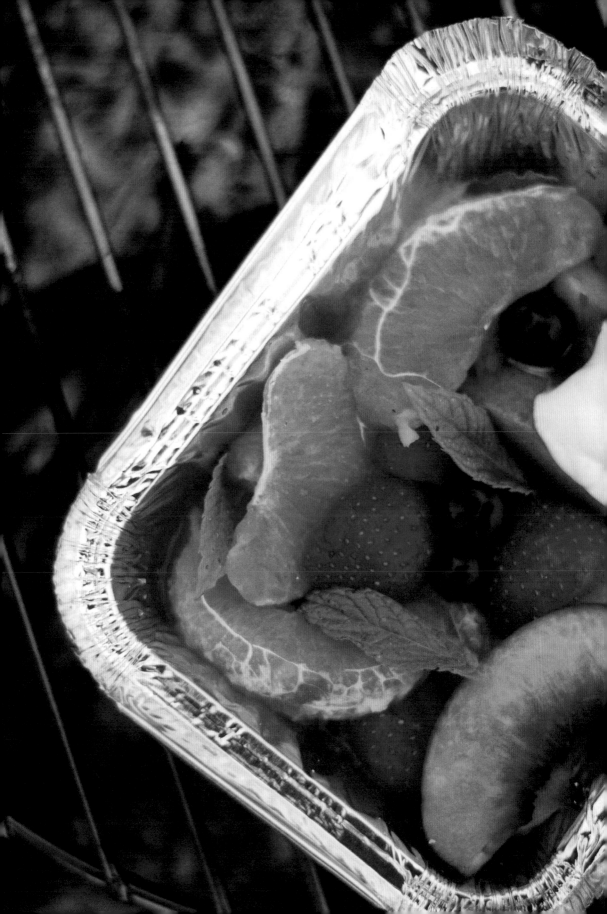

LIFE BEYOND THE
KITCHEN
WINDOW

If I were to tot up the hours spent at the kitchen sink they would amount to something quite substantial, however what I love about that time spent washing dishes is the view that I am treated to. In turn, this time spent scrubbing can feel less laboured and can sometimes be rather relaxing. Naturally, when the garden is in full bloom it is never more beautiful, however each season brings its beauty, which can be appreciated. Whatever the season, or the weather, the scene I love best is that of my feathered friends busily getting on with their day. We've had hens for many years, and recently have added some delightful ducks to the picture, which are especially lovely to watch on a rainy day. Those girls really make the most of the Irish weather. Hens are a wonderful addition to any garden, and I would definitely encourage anyone to get a few, if they have any available space.

No matter what the season, the view from the kitchen window will always include some foragable goods. A real love of mine is foraging for wild food, which is something that was a great part of my childhood. To forage for one's food has also become quite fashionable, with many top restaurants now promoting that they have their own in-house forager. I think this is truly fantastic. In the countryside we are surrounded by easily accessible free food, which turns out to be incredibly nutritious. Foraging, especially in the autumn months, is something that can easily be incorporated into a family walk.

I enjoy heading out to the garden, but my time always seems so limited, however I'm very lucky that my father is always around to keep an eye on the day-to-day growing of everything. My father came from a family that held a great passion for gardening, and this is something that I have yet to get the real bug for, but he has certainly passed it on to my sister Grainne. As a hard-working dairy farmer, each day brought as much work as the day before, so I always remember that time for gardening was limited for him. But at any chance he got, he would spend time rooting through his gardens. Whenever we would visit a park or a friend's house, never would he leave without some 'slips', which he would then try to successfully grow in his own soil. The garden that surrounds his house today is filled with memories, not only ones created there, but so many of the beautiful plants have an associated story from where they originated. I'm lucky to have this man as my 'head gardener', to share with me his knowledge and who takes such care of the garden. However he is never short of a few helpers. Each spring, when we are getting ready the beds for planting, we always leave an area free for the children to plant what they please. They all take great care of their garden. Each year the excitement that comes from seeing something on their plate that was once a tiny seed in their hand is truly marvellous.

For the most part I'm a pretty impatient gardener, and generally want relatively instant gratification when it comes to edible lovelies from the outdoors. With this in mind, herbs have worked wonderfully for me. Not a day passes but I will depend on some herb, which is guaranteed to transform any dish in my kitchen. The most commonly used kitchen herbs such as basil, thyme, rosemary, oregano, chives and mint are very easy to grow and thrive well in almost any type of soil, and also need very little watering. In my experience, the herbs planted in the garden yield a much greater harvest than those I try to maintain on the kitchen window-sill. However, herbs will survive quite well in pots on kitchen window-sills; they just need a little more attention than their outdoor comrades. When planting herbs outdoors it's best to wait until the threat of frost has passed, so in Ireland this can often be late spring or even early summer. Because of the amazing beneficial health properties that kitchen herbs possess, I've included some herbal tea combinations in the home nurse chapter.

Within the garden we have many different fruit bushes, which were only there about a year before we could avail of its fruit. Each summer I make a substantial amount of jam from this fruit, and it will see us well into the following year. I'd highly recommend the making of home-made jam, yet to buy the fruit from the supermarket makes it all rather expensive. If you love your home-made jams, the easiest, tastiest and cheapest route is to plant a few fruit bushes. They will invariably be much more economical. Each year I add an extra few, which make up for some of the older ones producing less as they grow old.

Each summer our garden is awash with berries and currants, and even though their uses are limitless I will inevitably turn most of them into jam.

The garden and even our lush green countryside all actually greatly benefit from our somewhat ghastly climate of, it sometimes seems, never ending rain. Something that also encourages plants to grow to their full potential is lots of good compost. When preparing the soil, in early spring, we give the garden a good covering of old, rotting cow manure. This stinks the place for a few days, but is like rocket fuel to the upcoming plants. We also rely on our own compost, made from daily kitchen waste, which is marvellous for scattering over the clay throughout the growing season. This compost is not only free, but it also actually saves our household some money, due to the fact that the waste to the landfill has been reduced.

Looking out the kitchen window to see a garden rich in fruit and vegetables is really wonderful, especially as most of what grows in my garden is there relatively maintenance free. There is so much potential for a nutritionally better and more economic diet available to us in our back gardens. I could only hope to encourage others to pick up the spade in early spring or add a few feathered friends to the family to make the most of the soil that surrounds our homes, as it really can make a difference to a family's lifestyle.

KEEPING HENS

When I was a child my family kept many hens, and even though most of the farm work rested with my father, the care of the hens rested with my mother. This seemed to be the case with most houses, as the hens were seen as an extension of the kitchen duties. My father tells me that when he was growing up each country house would have at least twenty-five hens. The eggs were used for the family's daily nutrition, and whatever eggs were surplus would then be brought into town and sold. The housewives were solely dependent on this money for running their kitchen and home. Chicks would also be raised, with the pullets being kept for laying purposes and the male chicks being raised for the table. Hens had a most valued role in these country households, and even though it would be difficult to run a house nowadays from selling eggs, these feathered creatures still deserve to be held in high esteem as they make a valuable addition to any household.

In recent years there has been a very impressive surge in people keeping these feathered friends on a domestic scale, and when you see the benefit to keeping them it's really not surprising. The advantages to having your own hens are enormous, but the fact that you will benefit from a daily delivery of the most scrumptious chemical-free, fresh eggs is certainly the most fundamental reason to having these beautiful birds in your back garden. The quality of your own back-garden eggs is incomparable to any shop-bought variety. Their superior flavour and texture is ever apparent, no matter what dish is made using them.

Hens aren't terribly difficult to care for, and can become a real family affair. While younger children love the daily collection of eggs, the keeping of hens can be a wonderful responsibility to delegate to an older child in the house. Jack has been in charge of our hens for the past couple of years. Like all children he loves to be trusted with some responsibility and gets a wonderful sense of accomplishment when his hens are happy clucking around the garden. The selling of the surplus eggs to family and friends can also make an attractive enticement to any young entrepreneur.

AN INTRODUCTION TO KEEPING HENS

Taking care of hens is very straightforward, but there are a few basic guidelines that should be adhered to. There are some great poultry breeders and sellers around the country so ensure you are buying from a reputable seller who has a certificate stating that the birds are disease-free. Most will be selling point-of-lay pullets, which will be just a couple of weeks shy of laying. Once they lay their first egg they can be called a hen. Before you buy your hens, first you must decide how many you need and then set up their home accordingly.

We currently have ten hens, but four hens will provide plenty of eggs for an average-sized family. Ready-made chicken coops come in all different sizes, and there are also portable hen-houses available that come with a very convenient attached chicken run. It simply depends on how much space you can allow for your hens, and I would advise you to provide as much as is reasonably available.

- There should be sufficient room provided for your flock.
- The house must protect against the elements but still be well ventilated.
- There must be an area for the hens to perch, as this is where they will sleep at night. It needs to be a foot or so from the ground.
- Straw makes for the perfect bedding for the hens, but shredded paper can also be used.
- At least one nesting box, filled with clean straw, should be provided. This will encourage the hens to lay indoors, providing you with nice clean eggs.
- Ensure that the hens always have access to fresh water.
- The house must keep out rodents and predators such as the fox, mink and stoats. It can be more difficult to guarantee the protection against predators when these ladies are out and about. If fencing an area for the hens a 2-metre fence with 15cm of fence dug into the ground should provide sufficient security. The hens always make a big fuss when anything new or different enters the garden, which immediately alerts our old Labrador to spring into detective mode and she duly scours the periphery of the garden till she catches the scent of whatever was prowling.
- The hen house should be cleaned out every week, but the nesting box may require fresh straw twice a week.

FEEDING TIME

Hens love scraps from the table, and certainly have a preference for cooked foods over raw ones. Leftover porridge, potato peels and cooked vegetables are among our hens' favourites, and these will be gobbled up much more quickly than their oats or layer's pellets. However, it is vital for a laying hen to be fed specially formulated feed of layer's mash / pellets. This is a mixture made up of wheat, maize, oats, barley, rye, vitamins and minerals and is available from all farm stores and many hardware stores. If not using organic pellets / mash it is most important to check that the feed is GM-free. A few handfuls of rolled oats is also an inexpensive and nutritious way to bulk up a hen's diet. The hens also need access to grass, of which they eat a lot, as well as some grit, such as small stones and gravel. This grit helps to grind the food in their stomachs and also provides the hen with a form of calcium, which will give strength to the shell of their eggs. At all times, the hens must have access to fresh water; each hen can drink up to a pint of water every day.

HOW TO KNOW IF A HEN IS SICK

Good sanitation and cleanliness are paramount for healthy hens. A clean coop as well as clean feeding equipment goes a long way in keeping your hens happy and healthy.
Hens are so sprightly and energetic it can be quite easy to spot if one in the flock is feeling under the weather. Generally they will be slow of movement and contain themselves in one area for a long period of time and they won't be interested in their food. The colour of their comb, being pink instead of red, can also be an indicator of a sick hen. They may also display some discharge from the nose and eyes. If you notice that some of the hens are eating more than normal and are laying very little there could be a chance that they have picked up round or tape worms. The vet can provide you with medication to treat worms, but dosing your flock twice a year is a good precautionary measure.

Each year, normally in early autumn, a hen will lose a lot of their feathers. This is called moulting, and lasts for about four weeks. During this time the hens won't lay, as the calcium needed to produce the eggs is temporarily being used for a new coat of feathers. If a hen is suffering from feather loss at another time of the year it could be an indication that it is unwell – just check for other signs of sickness. The contraction of salmonella can also be a risk for hens, but sending a sample of faeces and a dozen eggs to the local laboratory for testing can out rule any worry and only costs a few euros. Hens can also contract disease and infections from wild birds, so it's important that the hens' feeding area isn't accessible for these birds to feed from.

If at any time you are worried about the health of your hens, contact your vet, who will be best to advise on such matters. Over the past number of years I have lost a few hens, some which were being treated for a sickness, but in most cases it was sudden death. Only on bringing the first hen mortality to the local laboratory did I realise that in fact this service, of providing a post mortem on poultry, is free in Ireland. According to the laboratory it's a service that not many actually avail of. I think it is extremely important to know what the hen died from, if it was contagious and whether or not my remaining hens are at risk. Thankfully our own lovely hens are very rarely sick.

If ever I could recommend a step to self-sufficiency that is both practical and straightforward, then the keeping of a few hens would be it.

JAM MAKING

My mother was a talented jam maker, and each summer she would make enough jam to see us through the full year. When I was a child my parents had an acre of berries; raspberries, gooseberries but mostly strawberries, which they sold to passers-by and many local shops. The start of the season brought immense excitement, as not only were there juicy berries for the taking, but also our house would be aflood with traffic, which for a child makes for a much more entertaining summer than one spent playing / fighting with siblings. Whatever strawberries had been picked but were not sold would on that evening be made into the sweetest summer jam. Summer nights were spent preparing fruit and making jam of every variety. Now for the past number of summers I've had a great supply of my own fresh berries and currants. As much as I adore munching on fresh fruit, realistically no family could really go through a few kilos each day, for about a month. I will normally freeze quite a bit of it, as this means that I can have garden-fresh fruit all year round. However, in my opinion the best way to honour these juicy treasures all year round is by turning them into jam. Home-made jam is actually relatively easy to make, and the taste is just fantastic. If you are a novice at jam making, here are a few tips that may help you on the road to your own jammy delights.

221

- To sterilise jam jars hand wash and remove the labels then put them through a hot wash in the dishwasher. Alternatively, place the washed jars onto a baking tray and place into a warm, preheated oven at 140°C for 15 minutes. Even if the jars have been sterilised, I pop them into the warm oven for 5 minutes, to heat prior to filling with the hot jam.

- I tend to make small batches of jam, which are made more quickly and result in slightly fresher tasting jam.

- It's important to use fresh fruit that is dry and spotless. Don't use fruit that is bruised, mouldy or over ripe as these in turn will ruin the jam. Frozen fruit also makes perfect jam, once it was frozen in a perfectly fresh state.

- A large, wide saucepan is best for making jam as the fruit tends to cook more quickly and also more evenly.

- Heat the sugar in a casserole dish or stainless steel bowl, in a warm oven {140°C} for 15 minutes. This prevents the fruit from cooling with the addition of the sugar, which in turn would lengthen the cooking time, which takes from the jam's freshness.

❀ The white scum that rises to the top near the end of jam making can be skimmed away. A little knob of butter added after the jam has reached setting point will also help to dissolve some of this scum.

❀ To test that the jam is at setting point, place a saucer into the fridge before commencing the jam making. When the jam appears cooked, take the saucer from the fridge and put a teaspoonful of the jam onto the cold saucer. Leave for a minute, then if the jam wrinkles when pushed by a finger it is set. If not, return to the heat and repeat this process every 5 minutes until set. Alternatively, use a jam thermometer, and when it hits 105°–110°C the jam is at setting point.

❀ To pot the jam, pour into the sterilised jar, either using a ladle and funnel or a small jug, filling almost to the top.

❀ Cover the surface with a waxed paper disc, waxed side down, or some baking parchment, cut to size. Leave to cool completely before sealing with a lid or a cellophane disc and elastic band. When the jam is cold, to secure the cellophane tightly, dip into hot water the side of cellophane that will not be touching the jam jar and secure tightly with the elastic band. The heat from the water will help to create a vacuum for sealing the jar.

❀ Label the jam with what flavour it is and the date it was made.

❀ Store in a cool, dry cupboard for up to a year.

There are many scents and sounds that can guarantee a burst of childhood summer memories for me. Freshly cut grass and the distant sound of combine harvesters cutting silage are among these, but nothing is surer to remind me of hot summer nights than the sweet scent that fills the air when strawberries are bubbling on the stove. Strawberry jam was an absolute favourite of mine. When the first batch of the season was being made, a brown soda loaf would always be lifted from the oven for its first sampling and it never failed to taste spectacular.

Halfway through the season my mother would experiment with the flavours, adding different fruits to the plain strawberry base. One of her favourites was strawberry and apple. This recipe is based on that exact jam. As strawberries are low in pectin, their jam doesn't tend to set terribly well. This doesn't bother me, as the fresh flavours are so pungent I would lap it up either way. The addition of the apple aids with the setting of the jam, while lending a little welcomed tartness to the final sweet flavour. I love the addition of vanilla to many sweet dishes, and it works beautifully paired with the strawberries. The longer the jam is left unopened, the stronger the vanilla taste.

The distinctive strawberry flavour with the subtle vanilla tone makes this an irresistible jar of goodness to have to hand when a reminder of summer, especially a nostalgic childhood one, is needed.

VANILLA-INFUSED STRAWBERRY JAM

INGREDIENTS

1kg strawberries, hulled and quartered

1 granny smith apple, cored, peeled and coarsely grated

900g granulated Sugar

1 vanilla pod

METHOD

Preheat the oven to 200°C / fan 180°C / Gas Mark 6.

Put the strawberries and grated apple into a large, wide saucepan on a low heat.

Put the sugar in a stainless steel bowl or large baking tray and place it in the oven for 15 minutes, but give it a stir regularly to ensure that the sugar isn't caramelising.

As the berries begin to gain heat, smash them well with a masher, but leave some of the strawberries intact. Slit the vanilla pod in half and scrape the seeds into the strawberries, then add the pods.

Simmer for 2 minutes, then add the heated sugar. Stir well with a wooden spoon, helping to dissolve the sugar.

Increase the heat under the saucepan, and bring the jam to a boil, stirring regularly for about 25 minutes.

Skim away any white froth that has risen to the top of the pan. Scoop out the vanilla pods, which can be rinsed and dried to make some vanilla sugar at a later stage. Take from the heat immediately and pot into sterilised containers.

Makes three 1lb pots

Loganberry or raspberry jam is by far the easiest of jams to make, and lucky for me I happen to have a great glut of them, from the garden, each summer. I've always enjoyed the sweet-but-tartness of raspberry jam, however loganberry, even though very similar to the raspberry flavour, possesses a more delicate sweetness that makes its jam irresistible. If you can't get your hands on some loganberries, which I have rarely seen for sale, I would urge you to buy a few loganberry plants, if only for the jam you will be able to savour a couple of years from now.

If you have never made jam before, then raspberry or loganberry is the one to start with, as you'll have a jar made from a punnet of berries within 15 minutes flat.

LOGANBERRY / RASPBERRY JAM

INGREDIENTS

500g loganberries
  or raspberries

500g granulated sugar

METHOD

Preheat the oven to 200°C / fan 180°C / Gas Mark 6.

Put the berries into a large, wide saucepan on a low heat.

Put the sugar in a stainless steel bowl or large baking tray and place it in the oven for 15 minutes, but give it a stir regularly to ensure that the sugar isn't caramelising.

As the berries begin to gain heat and bubble, smash them a little with a masher. Simmer for 2 minutes then add the heated sugar.

Stir well with a wooden spoon, helping to dissolve the sugar.

Increase the heat under the saucepan, and bring the jam to a boil, stirring regularly for 10 minutes.

Skim away any white froth that has risen to the top of the pan. Take from the heat immediately and ladle into sterilised containers, using a funnel.

Cover with a waxed disc, and allow to cool completely before screwing a lid on tightly.

Makes two 1lb pots

I once had the misfortune of assuming that a quite beautiful little berry, which looked very unassuming, could be munched upon and enjoyed as one would with a grape. What a mistake that turned out to be, as once the toughened skin has been broken through, one is met with a blast of sourness certainly not pleasing to the palate. This tart fruit should never be dismissed, however, as it's this sourness that delivers such a very well balanced jam, when combined with the copious amounts of sugar, which is required for most jam recipes, regardless of the sweetness of the fruit. Green Gooseberry as the main component for me delivers a very satisfying jam, as it's not overly sweet, and therefore well suited dolloped over some cream on a sweet scone. I have a great love for the fragrant elderflowers, and as they are still in season when the gooseberries appear, their addition in the jam complements the tart berries perfectly.

GREEN GOOSEBERRY & ELDERFLOWER JAM

INGREDIENTS

1.5kg Gooseberries

500ml water

6 elderflower heads, tied in muslin

1.5kg granulated sugar

METHOD

Top, tail and wash the gooseberries then place into a large, wide saucepan with the water and the elderflowers.

Bring to the boil, then simmer gently stirring occasionally to prevent it from sticking, for 30 minutes.

Put the sugar in a stainless steel bowl or large baking tray and place it in the oven at 200°C / fan 180°C / Gas Mark 6. for 15 minutes. Give it a stir regularly to ensure that the sugar isn't caramelising.

Remove the elderflowers from the jam and add the warmed sugar. Stir until the sugar has dissolved, then boil rapidly for 10 minutes or until it reaches setting point.

Pot into hot, clean jars. Cover with a waxed disc, and allow to cool completely before screwing a lid on tightly.

Makes five 1lb pots

It's no great fate having a rhubarb plant at the back of any garden. My father insists that a stool of rhubarb must be obtained from a plant that has proven to be a good producer. It will take about a year or possibly two to settle into the soil and produce a good crop, but after this, for about twenty years, this little plant will provide enough rhubarb for the year long. Normally by early March our rhubarb plant starts to grow, and as the weeks go by, and more of it is picked, it grows at an accelerated rate. It is one fruit that comes into season well before anything else is even showing its existence in the back garden. Its leaves are slightly poisonous, so do not consume or leave for cows in a neighbouring field to eat.

What this one plant produces is much greater than its demand, so luckily it is a fruit that is freezer friendly. When sliced and bagged it can become a very convenient ingredient for an autumn crumble or winter tart. I always make a substantial amount of jam from it, as I find it rather popular. I quite like the tartness of rhubarb jam and find it is not only desirable on toast and scones but provides a very good balance to a luscious cream sponge.

RHUBARB & GINGER JAM

INGREDIENTS

1 kg rhubarb

1 lemon, zest and juice

1 kg granulated sugar

1 tsp ground ginger

METHOD

Wipe the rhubarb and cut into 2.5cm pieces. Zest the lemon into a bowl and then juice it.

In a large bowl, layer the rhubarb with the sugar, lemon zest and juice. Cover the bowl with cling film and leave to stand overnight.

On the following day, put the contents of the bowl into a large, wide saucepan that has been lightly greased. Add the ground ginger. Steadily bring to the boil, stirring regularly, until it is a thick consistency, which will take about an hour.

Test if the jam has reached setting point.

Skim the white froth from the jam, and allow to cool slightly.

Carefully ladle the jam, using a funnel to help, into hot, clean jars.

Cover with a waxed disc, and allow to cool completely before screwing a lid on tightly. Store in the fridge or a dry, airy cupboard.

Makes four 1lb pots

Drying out tomatoes is a wonderful way to preserve some summer fruits while greatly intensifying their flavour. There are so many uses for sun-blushed tomatoes; they are a great addition to pasta dishes and sandwiches. One of my favourite uses for sun-blushed tomatoes is to chop up a few and add them, along with some fresh herbs, to my soda bread dough. While this bread is baking, the house is filled with wonderful scents of summer.

SUN-BLUSHED TOMATOES

INGREDIENTS

1kg fresh tomatoes

1tsp sea salt

A few grinds of
  black pepper

3 sprigs fresh thyme

2tsp sugar {only if the
  tomatoes aren't sweet}

Drizzle of olive oil, plus
  extra for storing.

METHOD

Preheat the oven to 160°C / fan 140°C / Gas Mark 3.

Slice the tomatoes and place tightly together on a baking tray.

Sprinkle over the salt, pepper, thyme leaves and sugar {if required}.

Drizzle with some olive oil.

Place in the oven for approximately 1½–2 hours, checking near the end of cooking to ensure that they are not burning. They will have shrivelled up a little but won't yet be charred.

Allow to cool before placing in an airtight container, drizzling with some olive oil and storing in the fridge for up to a month.

Even with our recent poor-weathered summers, the tomatoes in our greenhouse grow incredibly well. Near the end of the tomato season, the ripening process can slow down, but normally placing the greener ones in a paper bag along with a ripe banana can speed up the tomato's maturation. I came up with this recipe a few years ago, when I happened to have a large glut of tomatoes, which all ripened around the same time. I make many types of chutney and preserves each year, but this is the most requested jar from all the family. I've tried handing out the recipe, but to little avail, as I still have a long request list for this sauce year on year.

It is a cross between a chutney and a dipping sauce, and there seems to be very little that this little jar of goodness doesn't complement. It's scrumptious smothered over toasties, grilled meat or fish, but I like it most when served with crackers and a few chunks of my favourite cheese.

SWEET CHILLI TOMATO SAUCE

INGREDIENTS

700g ripe tomatoes

2 small red chillies, roughly chopped

4 cloves of garlic, crushed

200ml balsamic vinegar

500g caster sugar

Salt and freshly ground pepper

METHOD

To peel the tomatoes, score the top of each tomato with a cross. Boil a kettle full of water and pour it into a large heatproof bowl. Add the tomatoes for 30 seconds, then drain off the water, remove the tomatoes to a chopping board and peel back the skin from each one.

Place the chillies and garlic into a blender and blitz well. Add the peeled tomatoes and blitz for a further minute. If making by hand, chop the tomatoes, chillies and garlic very finely.

In a saucepan, over a medium heat, add the balsamic vinegar and the caster sugar. When the sugar is dissolved, tip in the tomato, garlic and chilli mixture. Season with salt and pepper.

Turn up the heat. Bring to the boil then simmer for 25 minutes. Take off the heat and allow to cool slightly, before pouring into sterilised pots.

Makes two 1lb pots

COMPOST

Composting is a wonderful way to make good use out of everyday household and garden waste. In many areas, brown composting bins are available from the council, which is marvellous, as it is a great saving for the homeowner. Composting can take as much as 30% of your household waste, saving you a lot of money on refuse charges. However, having your own compost bin / pile in your back garden brings even greater advantages, as you not only save money on waste but you will also get to benefit from what your compost bin produces. Making your own composts produces a natural, chemical-free, nutrient-rich fertiliser for your garden and lawn.

Where is it best to place the compost bin?

- Position the compost bin on grass or soil. This will allow the very important earthworm access to the compost, which will help with the process of breaking down the materials and also help to keep some air circulating.
- Even though the compost bin needs to be near to the house for easy access, if possible place it some distance away to avoid contamination. Be aware that it can sometimes smell.
- Place the bin in a sunny spot, as the heat will help with the composting process.

What can go into the compost bin?

- Many kitchen scraps make an important addition to the compost bin, as they are high in nitrogen and this helps to heat the compost, which in turn speeds up the whole composting process. These include: crushed eggshells, fruit and vegetable peels, tea bags, coffee grounds and flowers. I keep a container with a lid beside the sink and one of the children brings it to the compost bin every evening.
- Newspaper and light cardboard, shredded or cut into small pieces.
- Clean sawdust, not in one clump but dispersed through the pile.
- Garden waste such as grass clippings and leaves.
- Hair. If you do a little home barbering, dispose of the hair in the compost bin.
- Hen manure is an excellent compost activator.
- Straw and hay.
- Seaweed, rinsed, can add some valuable minerals to a compost bin.

What cannot be composted?

- Meat, bones, fish scraps or any cooked foods; these will attract pests.
- Diseased plants and weeds.
- Glass or plastic.
- Coloured or glossy paper.
- Pet litter
- Coal or charcoal

How can I help the composting process?

- Ensure that all that is added to the compost bin is small, as this will help to speed up the production of the compost. Chop or shred any large materials.
- It's important to keep the compost pile aerated. Mix the contents regularly with a spade to introduce oxygen to the pile, which will help the materials to break down.
- A good mix of dry and wet materials layered into the pile will help with a speedier production of compost. Do not put in too much of any one material.

With very little maintenance, within 4–6 months your own nutrient-rich compost will be ready to use.

Before modern meteorology, 'the old crowd', as my father would call them, had their own ways of forecasting the weather. According to them, nature had its own way of predicting what was in store for the coming season. Even though my father always had a great interest in nature, it was my mother who, without fail, would bring me foraging each and every week of autumn. I can clearly remember my mother coming back from one of our walks with the report to my father that the hedgerows were flush with rosehips. He quoted the old proverb, "Many Hips & Haws – Many Frosts & Snaws", and sure enough that winter we had one of the heaviest snow falls for years.

Rosehips are jewel-like beads that decorate the hedgerow in early to mid-autumn.

They are high in Vitamin C as well as a rich source of Vitamins A, D and E.

This syrup has many uses. It makes a very effective vitamin tonic, and is also delicious diluted with water for a nutritious, refreshing drink. I often serve rosehip syrup in place of maple syrup, drizzled over ice-cream or pancakes.

ROSEHIP SYRUP

INGREDIENTS

500g rosehips,
   topped & tailed &
   roughly chopped

1 litre of water

300g caster sugar

METHOD

Wash the rosehips and chop finely.

In a saucepan, bring the water to the boil and add the rosehips. Boil for 10 minutes, then take from the heat and cover with the lid, allowing the rosehips to infuse for 20 minutes.

Strain through a fine sieve into a clean saucepan. Add the sugar, stir well and boil for 5 minutes.

Pour into sterilised bottles or jars and seal the lid tight. Store in the fridge.

HOME-MADE CORDIALS

Water is naturally the best drink that any of us could choose, but sometimes it can be a little difficult to convince a child that boring old water is the superior option to the tasty sugary 'fruit' drink. Home-made cordials can solve some of these issues. The best time to make them is during the summer months, when fruit is plentiful. I normally make large batches of cordials as they keep perfectly in the refrigerator for several months.

My favourite cordial of all is made using beautiful fragrant elderflowers. These blossoms are in full bloom in early summer, when their floral fragrance fills the countryside. There are many uses for this versatile cordial. Its perfumed sweet flavour is a lovely addition to many desserts, and complements tart berries, especially gooseberries, when used as part of a crumble or tart. Most often it is used as the base of a deliciously refreshing drink when diluted with water, white wine or champagne.

ELDERFLOWER CORDIAL

INGREDIENTS

15 elderflower heads

1.2 kg granulated sugar

900ml water

2 lemons

METHOD

Shake the elderflowers to expel any dirt or insects, and place just the heads into a large bowl.

Dissolve the sugar in the water, and bring to the boil for 2 minutes. Remove from the heat and allow to cool for 15 minutes.

Zest the lemons, and then thinly slice them before adding both zest and slices to the elderflowers in the bowl.

Add the sugary syrup. Combine all the ingredients then cover with cling film. Leave overnight, at room temperature, to infuse.

The next day, strain the syrup through a muslin-lined sieve into clean bottles. Store in the fridge ready to use.

Blackcurrants are a rich antioxidant and are extremely high in Vitamin C. They actually contain 5 times the amount of Vitamin C that is found in an average orange. A 100g serving of blackcurrants contain a staggering 302% of an adult's daily requirement of Vitamin C. They are also a good source of fibre, potassium, phosphorous and iron. Such a small little fruit, but it packs a mighty health punch. As with most fruits, the cooking processes will somewhat reduce the nutritional count in the blackcurrants, but even then this cordial is still bursting with vitamins. My children enjoy it best when diluted with water and served ice-cold, but it can also be deemed the perfect tonic for a sore throat when added to some hot water and honey.

BLACKCURRANT CORDIAL

INGREDIENTS

500g blackcurrants

2lt water

Zest & juice of 1 lemon

500g granulated sugar

METHOD

Place the blackcurrants and water into a large saucepan. Add the zest and juice of a lemon.

Bring to the boil and simmer for 15 minutes.

Strain the contents of the saucepan through a sieve into another clean saucepan.

Add the sugar to the hot liquid. Stir well, and when the sugar has dissolved bring to the boil for 3 minutes.

Pour into sterilised bottles and seal well. When fully cooled, place in the refrigerator.

Dilute with water or sparkling water to taste and serve with lots of ice.

I always thought that home-made liqueurs sounded rather ominous, but also somewhat intriguing. I generally believed that dabbling in such a production would be limited to some secret home-brewing club, but alas it appears that the making of home-made liqueurs really couldn't be easier. Many combinations of fruit and alcohol will work, but a great opportunity to give it a try is when blackberries are in full season and they are scattered through the countryside free for the taking. Blackberries, sugar, vodka, and ideally a Kilner jar, are all that is needed for creating this deliciously sweet liqueur, which could be drunk with just ice or as a rather impressive pudding ingredient. The joy with blackberry vodka is that it is made in the autumn, which means it will be perfect for using just in time for Christmas. After straining the vodka, an added bonus are the beautifully preserved blackberries, which are perfect to be used in a Christmas pudding mixture or simply served over pancakes with a dollop of yogurt as a very grown up breakfast treat.

BLACKBERRY VODKA

INGREDIENTS

250g blackberries

125g caster sugar

400ml vodka

METHOD

Sterilise a Kilner jar {see page} or a wide-necked jar.

Very carefully wash the blackberries, then dry using a paper towel.

Place the blackberries in the jar and top with the sugar. Pour over most of the vodka.

Close the lid and gently shake the jar, helping the sugar to dissolve and topping up with the vodka as it sinks into the berries.

Place the jar in a cool, dark place and take it out daily, for the first 2 weeks, to give it a little shake. After this, just give it a shake once a week for 6 weeks. The blackberry vodka can then be left at the back of a dark press for another few weeks.

When ready to use, strain the vodka into another sterilised bottle or jar and reserve the berries, which can be used as part of a dessert or popped into a glass as a tasty addition to a blackberry-based cocktail. The strained blackberry vodka can be kept in a cool, dark place for 1 year.

STINGING NETTLE SOUP

Growing up on a farm, I spent a lot of my day out in the fields and endured many a nettle sting. Who knew that all those times I cursed upon nettles that one day I'd be enjoying them as one of the countryside's most valuable ingredients. For most, the only association one will hold with nettles is the memory of a stinging leg or forearm, after unknowingly encountering a plant, so possibly to think of upgrading this plant of nemesis to a worthy ingredient may be a bit of a struggle. However, on hearing of its impressive nutritional content I couldn't shy away from giving them a try.

Nettles are extraordinary high in iron and are also rich in Vitamins A, C, K, Calcium and Potassium. Nettles have been used, for their medicinal value, since medieval times, when they were used primarily as a diuretic. The first time I made this soup was when my father was feeling the effects of a low iron count. Wherever possible I was eager to include iron-rich foods in his diet, so on learning about the benefits of cooking with nettles I decided it was worth picking a few to make what I could with them.

Dad had memories of nettle soup from his childhood, so he was enthusiastic to revisit the taste, and thankfully my updated version didn't disappoint. The making of this soup very much reminds me of that old fable of stone soup. The base is clearly a leek and potato, but with the addition of a few handfuls of nettles this intriguing title is obtained. The sting of the nettle is lost once it encounters the hot fluid, but somehow this soup still brings a pleasing after-taste and a feeling of tingling to the tongue.

The best time to pick nettles is late spring / early summer when there is fresh young growth on the plants. Make sure to pick from plants that are organic, ensuring that they are far from anywhere that may have been sprayed with a weed-killer. Also, be sure to wear thick gardening gloves when you pick nettles to avoid any unnecessary stings. If you are short on time, and need a quick and easy nutritional boost, nettles actually make a very refreshing tea, especially when paired with a little fresh mint. In fact, with any recipe that requires spinach or leafy greens, nettles can be used in their place. This soup is completely delicious and very nutritious.

STINGING NETTLE SOUP

INGREDIENTS

150g young nettles, washed & chopped

50g butter

250g potatoes, peeled and cut into 1cm cubes

110g leeks, white and light green parts only, chopped

110g onion, chopped

Salt & freshly ground pepper

900ml chicken or vegetable stock

1 tbsp of fresh sage, chopped finely

125ml cream / milk

METHOD

Start by preparing the nettles. To remove the sting from the nettles, place them in a saucepan or heatproof bowl and cover them with boiling water. Allow to sit for one minute, then drain. Discard the stems and roughly chop the leaves only.

Melt the butter in a heavy saucepan. Add the potatoes, leeks and onions and toss in the butter until well coated.

Sprinkle with salt and a few grinds of pepper. Cover with the butter wrapper or a piece of greaseproof paper and place the lid back on the saucepan. Sweat over a gentle heat for about 10 minutes until the vegetables are softer but not coloured.

Discard the butter wrapper, add the stock and bring to the boil. Reduce the heat and simmer for about 10 minutes, until all the vegetables are cooked.

Add the chopped nettle leaves and sage. Simmer for a couple of minutes with the lid off the saucepan.

Add the cream or milk and liquidise the soup in a blender or food processor. Taste and adjust the seasoning if necessary. Reheat and serve.

Serves 6

One of my favourite and most convenient ingredients to have to hand is pesto. A dollop over some cooked pasta makes the perfect quick snack, while a spoonful of pesto can give the finishing touches to dishes that are in need of a little more than just seasoning. A few years ago on tasting some wild garlic pesto I declared that I must seek out some of this wild plant to make a batch of pesto for myself. My searches brought me to typical places where wild garlic should reside, such as wooded areas and close to streams. After a long day of searching for wild garlic, I was very proud to bring home what I had gathered. My father-in-law took note of my gatherings, only to declare that the back hedge of their back garden was heavily laden with these large leafy growths. As much of a learning curve as my day foraging had been, I've been relieved each season since to simply pop over to my parents-in-law's house and fill the boot with lots of lovely wild garlic leaves.

If you haven't been in contact with wild garlic before there is no mistaking its identity, as when bruised its scent is so distinctively garlic. Pesto can be expensive to make, therefore being able to avail of the main ingredient for free is fantastic. It's worth searching out some wild garlic as its pungent garlic flavour is perfect for pesto, and especially since what you will make isn't even available to buy in most supermarkets.

WILD GARLIC PESTO

INGREDIENTS

50g wild garlic leaves

25g basil leaves

25g pine nuts

½ a garlic clove,
  peeled and crushed

200ml olive oil

50g parmesan cheese,
  finely grated

Salt and freshly
  ground pepper

METHOD

Using a food processor, blend for a few seconds the wild garlic, basil, pine nuts, garlic and olive oil. If using a pestle and mortar, pound all these ingredients together.

Place in a bowl, and stir in the parmesan. Taste and season with a little salt and pepper. Pour into a sterilised jar and top with a little extra olive oil.

To prolong its shelf life, each time after using, clean the top and inside of the jar and top with a little extra olive oil.

Makes 350ml

INDEX

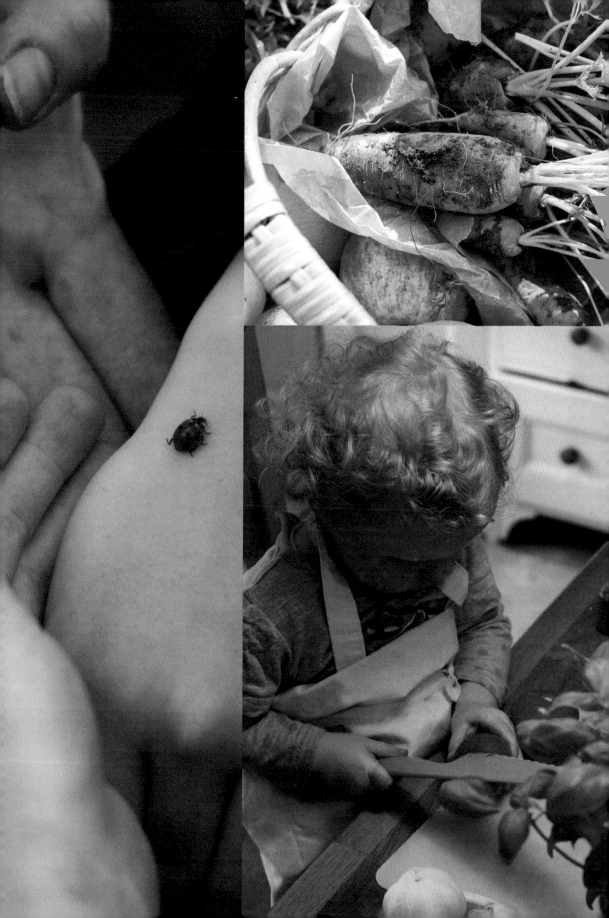